A Sin
Being and Time

by
Steven Foulds

ISBN 13: 978-1494829711
ISBN 10: 1494829711

For US readers: This Guide is prepared in New Zealand English which differs from US English in some of its spelling.

Also by Steven Foulds from *Amazon*:

<u>Philosophy</u>. *A Serious Guide to Being and Time* (e-book and paperback), *BEING REAL* (e-book and paperback), *Religion* (e-book).

<u>Novels</u>. *Fragments of Truth from the Fictions of a Self* (e-book and paperback), *Whispers from the Prison of Fact* (e-book), *Boredom* (e-book).

The Renovation Philosophy and Mythology Page (<u>www.hinau.co.nz</u>).

Table of Contents

1. Getting Started

When Martin Heidegger published *Sein und Zeit* (*Being and Time*) in 1927, the published text was intended to be the foundation of a three-part inquiry into the meaning of Being. As it happened, history intervened and the projected Parts Two and Three weren't published. But Heidegger's need to clarify the Being of human persons in his foundation, as a way of 'getting at' the meaning of Being, has left us with a truly revolutionary insight into what it is to be a person.

Roughly speaking, **Being** is the meaningful character of some entity; here is a tree being what it is, there is a cow being what it is, and so on. This means that the only way to get at the meaning of Being is to interrogate [examine] some entity. The lives of persons are entities that lend themselves to such interrogation because, in living the life of a person, we deal with Being directly. A snail, for example, may crawl all over a hammer, a cat may sniff it and a dog may piss on it, but only persons deal with its Being as a hammer, that is, its meaningful character as a tool having a particular function in the world. Naturally enough, the only persons accessible to interrogation by Heidegger were human. The **human** aspect of a human person is an animal of the species *homo sapiens*. Being human is not the subject of *Being and Time* because it is not the human part of the human person that discloses the Being of entities. Being a **person**, however, is something that humans do; it's a way of relating to the world understandingly. In *Being and Time* Heidegger interrogates the activity of being a person [**there-being**] because only that activity discloses

Being (*using* a hammer *as a hammer*, for instance, discloses the Being of the hammer, and the Being of a person, in a way that seeing, touching, hearing, smelling or taking it apart does not).

Disclosedness is a matter of revealing the Being of something. You disclose the Being of a hammer, for instance, when you understand it as (1) 'fitting in' to, and having significance for, the 'overall scheme of things' which is the world, and (2) having certain possibilities for use in various projects that have to do with existing in one way or another. Only persons can disclose a hammer *as* a hammer or a tree *as* a tree, not in the sense of giving them names but as grasping their significance as part of the world. As only persons can do this, and as doing this is necessary for being a person, disclosedness is a basic and essential[1] aspect of there-being.

The Being of entities, including ourselves, matters to persons, but our own Being as persons is itself not clear to us, and Heidegger devotes a lot of *Being and Time* to making the Being of human persons clear. The biggest barrier to doing this is not ignorance but misunderstanding - especially in the form of flawed historical assumptions. For thousands and thousands of years, humans have tried to understand themselves as a special kind of thing that is placed in a world of other things. This myth obscures the truth that being a person is not a matter of being a soul or mind or whatever but of undertaking

---

1. Heidegger uses the term translated 'essential' in its literal sense of 'that without which an entity could not be the entity it is'.

a particular activity in the world over time. It is the activity of being a person in the world and over time which Heidegger interrogates [analyses] as 'there-being.'

There-being [being a person] is an activity over time that involves engaging with the world in terms of possibilities for existing in different ways - as a builder, teacher, criminal, layabout, patriot, farmer, or whatever. Because these possibilities are open to you, and you have to constantly be choosing at least one at the expense of others, you care about them and who you are being is a issue for you. The way you *act* over time, as a potentiality to whom possibilities in the world matter, discloses there-being (brings it into view).

The concept of there-being - the way that (in our case, human) persons go about doing what persons do when they are being persons - replaces the traditional thingish notions of personhood. It would be hard to overestimate just how radical and important this change is. If, like most humans, you dichotomize Being into material and immaterial aspects then you are likely to think of the essence of your personhood as some sort of soul, mind, consciousness, or whatever. And you may well be challenged by the fact that this thing-like core of you cannot be found and/or that, if you do try to reduce the core of personhood to biology or physics, the reduction fails to account for the reality of being a person as you experience it. If, however, you carefully observe your actual experience of being a person, without making any prior religious or scientific assumptions, you may notice that being a person is something that you are doing. What you are doing cannot be discovered by taking a brain apart - dissecting all or any part of the human body is interrogating the wrong evidence in the wrong way.[2]

If you dichotomise your personhood from the world then (a) each could be what it is without the other but (b) we have no adequate explanation of how they interact (how, for example, does the 'mind' interact with the brain?). This ancient and enduring dichotomy is, however, false. Just as you could not be a teacher in the absence of possibilities for teaching, or could not be honest in the absence of possibilities for telling the truth or lying, so you could not undertake the activity of being a person in the absence of possibilities for undertaking that activity. Whatever provides those possibilities is a **world**. So a world of some kind, and a particular kind of *integrity* of the world and being in it, is necessary for being a person.

The traditional picture of a person as some kind of soul, consciousness or other thing-like essence, obscures the truth that (1) you need a world in which to be a person, (2) a particular way of being in the world is essential to being a person, and (3) the Being of the world, its components, *and yourself*, is an issue for you.

Being is an issue for persons because being a person entails constantly facing possibilities for living in different ways. A cat

---

2. Dissecting anything doesn't disclose its Being so much obscure it (close it off). Even something as simple as a hammer loses its Being as a hammer (stops being a tool for banging things) if you dissect it into a head and a handle.

doesn't concern itself with being one kind of cat or another, a tree doesn't concern itself with choosing a way of life, but persons do concern themselves with being certain kinds of persons (a builder, liar, entertainer, thief, parent, rich, popular, brave, and so on). This is because, unlike cats or trees, we not only can but have to choose a way of life from a range of limited but real possibilities. In choosing a way of life, you are continually faced with possibilities from among which you can choose and, at each choice, you actualise at least one of the possibilities available to you while thereby waiving others (telling lies, for instance, waives the possibility of being honest). You have to iterate these choices constantly - being honest this morning doesn't in the least remove the possibility of being dishonest this afternoon. So living the life of a person is a matter of continually choosing a possible way of life in the world - if you are going to be an honest person then you have to keep on choosing to be honest at every opportunity have for being honest or dishonest. Added to this, the Being of everything in your world is an issue for you because various actualities and possibilities are threats or resources to the way of life you are choosing. Only persons, for example, deal with hammers as tools for building or committing murder depending on what kind of life they are choosing to live.

The difference between entities that are being persons, and those that are not, can be brought out by comparing the essences of each. The **essence** of any entity is that without which it could not be the entity it is. **The essence of things** is a set of material or conceptual structures. **The essence of being a person**, however, is a way of relating to possibilities from among which you choose some at the expense of others. This way of relating to the world is **existence**. Existence is more than the life of a human animal because all that is essential for life are certain integrated biological processes. The process of being a person, however, requires particular kinds of ongoing engagements with the sorts of possibilities that only a world can provide. In observing that the essence of there-being is existence, Heidegger points out that no plant or animal can be a person unless it is engaging with a world in a certain way. What is essential to being a person is not a set of thingish properties, such as having a mind or hominid biology, but a particular way of engaging with a world. In Heidegger's terminology, inanimate objects *are*, animals, plants and persons *live*, but only persons *exist*.

It follows from all this that the Being of persons [there-being] can be disclosed only in terms of existence; scientific, psychological, evolutionary, sociological, or other, facts about what human persons are is the wrong evidence to interrogate if we want to get at our Being as persons. Analysing existence is far different from analysing things. Thingish analysis is **categorial**; you may categorise people physically, for example, as thin, fat, hairy, sexy, Polynesian, tall, male, young, and so on. This narrates what the object is by placing its characteristics in various categories. Such classification could describe your facts in exhaustive detail, and have all its details true, without even beginning to describe how you go about existing as a person in the world. This means that, as well as thing-like categories to clarify what you are as a human, you need another kind of categorisation to make clear the process by which you go about being a person. This kind of categorisation is 'existential' - a word which obviously derives from 'existence.'

The term '**existential**' refers to the common structures or logic of existence [living the life of a person in the world and over time]. Where the sciences undertake a categorial analysis of human persons, Heidegger undertakes an existential analysis of the process of being a person (i.e., he interrogates existentiality). The terms 'existential' and 'existentiality' always have to do with existing in a certain way in a world and over time. Classes of existential possibility are called '**existentialia**.' Heidegger distinguishes the common existential features of there-being, not only from the categorial features of what things are but also from the existentiell features of an individual's particular existence. Where existential features are common to the existence of all persons; **existentiell** features are specific to a particular individual's existence. So, for example, the fact that reading books is a possible human way of being a person is an existential fact of human there-being; the fact that you are reading this book is an existentiell fact about your existence. In *Being and Time*, Heidegger is not after the existentiell features of a given existence but the existential features of being a person that are common across the globe because it is these that he believes will disclose the meaning of Being.

Obviously you cannot live the life of a person - existing in various possible ways - unless you are engaging with an environment in which possibilities for existing in various ways can be found and actualised. Whether this environment is material or 'spiritual' is irrelevant - just as fish need water in which to live the lives of fish, so persons need a world in which to live the lives of persons. Normally, when humans set out to study their own Being, they do so by considering it in their own cultural environment. This is misleading because the special features of being Austrian, tribal, Hindu, urban, or whatever, are limited rather than truly existential. It is, therefore, the **average everydayness** that is common to virtually all human lives in various times and cultures which Heidegger observes.

An Introductory Overview of There-being

Humans exist as persons by repeatedly choosing possibilities for existing with at least some understanding that actualising different possibilities is significant for being whatever kind of person they are choosing to be. So whereas all sparrows, for example, build and maintain similar nests all over the world, persons design, build, buy or rent, shelters of many different kinds, neglect or care for them to different degrees, and contribute to the realisation of the kinds of person they are by the kind of shelter they choose to design, build and live in.

This explains the necessity of using a particular kind of (existential) analysis to get at the Being of persons. The key to this analysis is that, 'In determining itself as an entity, there-being always does so in the light of a possibility which is itself and which, in its very Being, it somehow understands.' There are two kinds of possibility at stake here.

- A **categorial possibility** - which is the kind of possibility that things have - is a state of 'could be but isn't yet'. As an ontological category applied to things, possibility is grouped with actuality and impossibility.
- An **existential possibility** - which is the kind of possibility that you *are* - is an aspect of there-being whereby persons are possible builders or destroyers, possible saints or slobs, possibly cruel or kind, and so on. As animals, humans have a fixed nature which determines their way of life as air-breathing, omnivorous, bi-pedal, mammalian and so on. As persons, however, humans not have a fixed character that determines their existence. You were not, for example, born honest or dishonest in such a way that you have to live an honest or dishonest life; you are a potential liar or honest person and *make* yourself one or the another by telling lies or telling the truth (i.e., you choose a possible existence which gives you an actual nature). This means not only that the world is a world of possibilities to persons but that you yourself are 'possibility incarnate' - in Heidegger's terminology, your Being as an existential [living] possibility is that of **potentiality-for-being**.

The categorial possibilities of things derives from the existential possibilities [potentiality-for-being] of persons; a rock is a possible tool or weapon, for instance, only because persons are potential builders and fighters. Choosing to exist in one way or another thereby determines a character; you become a parent, music teacher, or whatever, by existing as [living the life of] a parent, music teacher, and so on. If you are not a musician then you may not fully appreciate that you are a potential musician who can make herself or himself an actual musician by making music. Nevertheless, you 'somehow understand' that you are always choosing from among your possibilities for existing in one way or another according to the relevance of those possibilities for being one kind of person or another.

That persons are potentialities-for-being, who need ongoing possibilities to actualise simply to exist as persons, is one of the key insights of *Being and Time*. This insight matters particularly because humans chronically misdefine their Being as persons in terms of actualities - who you are is thought to be fixed by your biological or 'spiritual' constitution, race, gender, star sign, career, social class, or whatever. In doing this we think of persons as things - and so cover up our own there-being as persons.[3]

Traditionally, humans have tried to analyse personhood **categorially**; the supposed Being of this person is explained as belonging to the categories human, woman, urban, sexually mature, extroverted, Fijian, middle class, endomorphic, 'sagittarian', and so on. This doesn't work for an entity whose essence is existence; an existential analysis must categorise existence in terms of **existentialia**; that is, in sets of

---

3. I put the word 'spiritual' in scare quotes not just because its use is confused and dubious but also because I have come to suspect that the many ways in which it is tossed around is seriously interfering with our understanding of reality. Indeed, I strongly suspect that the whole 'spiritual or material' dichotomy is seriously wrong-headed and should simply be abandoned.

possibilities. For example, the possibilities that range from existing honestly to existing dishonestly is an **existentiale** (singular) because only persons can and must choose to exist in or between one of these ways and the other. Each existentiale includes a range of possible existences from among which each person chooses one at the expense of not choosing the others. Consider, for instance, the range of lived attitudes that go from being honest to being dishonest. A rock, tree, cow or motorbike cannot be said to be either honest or dishonest, but (1) every person is always existing somewhere on the honest-to-dishonest scale and (2) you can be dishonest only at the expense of honesty and *vice versa*. This makes the honest-dishonest range of possibilities an existentiale.

2. Being-In-The-World

The difference between categorial and existential analysis is immediately obvious if we want to understand the world within which persons exist. Categorially, the world is just a collection of things in space and time. Existentially, however, **the world** is the 'workshop' or 'wherein'[4] in which you go about the business of existing in one way or another. To persons, the world is meaningful, and it is only because persons exist in the world that is has meaning and matters to them. This meaning derives from existence. The weather, for example, doesn't have any intrinsic meaning of itself but is meaningful, and can be understood, because it affects the existence of beings whose existence demands understanding.

> Throughout *Being and Time* the term 'world' always applies to the existential (meaningful) world.

Traditional (categorial) human notions of being a person detach us from the world - you just happen to be placed as a thing among things in much that same way as items on a shelf or water in a glass. This makes being in the world something secondary to being a person (as when a 'soul' is said to be reincarnatable in the way that water can be poured from one glass to another without affecting its essential character as water). The world and persons are, in this case, merely

---

4. A **wherein** is the place of an activity. A kitchen, for example, is the wherein of preparing food to eat (see also *region*).

alongside each other. This categorial idea of 'being in' does not apply to being-in-the-world as a person. **Being-in-the-world** is an intimate engagement with the possibilities that are manifest in the world *when persons are being-in it, to persons being-in it* and *by persons being-in it* - an engagement which is necessary for existence and defines the world as a world [the 'wherein' of existence]. The phrase 'being-in-the-world' is hyphenated to reflect the essential integrity of existing and the world in which you exist - matter, energy, space and time constitute a world [a meaningful integrity] only because persons exist in them, and persons can exist in them only because they constitute a world. You have to exist [live the life of a person over time] somewhere; this existence is not in your mind or whatever but in the world. It is, moreover, a lived and intimate *engagement* with the world. In the same way that you simply cannot exist as a driver without driving something, or as a gardener without growing something, so you cannot exist as a person without engaging with a world. This is because existing is, like driving or gardening, an activity that can be undertaken only over time and only by variously exploiting or neglecting the possibilities which only a world can provide. Only in a world where both lying and being honest are possible, for example, can you make yourself honest or dishonest by existing honestly or dishonestly. The idea that you could be 'essentially' honest, without living an honest life, is incoherent. You create an honest or dishonest character for yourself by being-in-*the-world* and *by being-in-*the-world.

You can illustrate how your being-in-the-world is different from a thing's being in the world by thinking of touch. To say that two things touch each other is just a measure of geographic proximity. There is nothing meaningful to either thing in that touch. To a person, however, the touch of a lover, the touch of a parent or child, or the touch of a knife held to a throat, are meaningful. In all of your senses you encounter items in the *world* - not in your head. You do this because they are relevant to your existence; you deal with tables as surfaces on which to place things, you encounter and use assertions about the world as tools or weapons that are relevant to what you want out of life, and so on. So, for persons, the objects in the world are not just actual matter and energy but possible assets or liabilities - you concern yourself with them.

Concern is an aspect of **Care**; that is, a range [existentiale] of related attitudes deriving from the fundamental fact that facts, and the possibilities they represent, all matter to you in various ways - you desire or fear them, value them highly, or couldn't care less. Calling the Being of there-being 'Care' does not imply that persons are always caring but only that we are always variously caring *or* careless whereas a wall or footpath, for example, is neither. This existentiale, which arises from the fact that Being is a issue for you, is expressed as, and explains, all the other aspects of your being-in-the-world.

Care has two aspects: **concern** [when *states of affairs* matter to you] and **solicitude** [when *persons* matter to you]. Both of these are your relationships with objects - things and persons respectively - according to their relevance for your existence.

The use of the word 'concern', for instance, does not imply that persons always take care of objects but only that they matter to us in various ways that reflect their relevance to how we are variously living our lives as persons in the world. Being concerned with various objects of attention - even if you are not concerned about their welfare - is an essential character of being-in-the-world as a person. Like all existentialia, including solicitude, concern covers a range of possibilities - in this case, having to do with being variously concerned about or indifferent to objects. So Care-related ways of dealing with objects in the world include not only concern-for but also indifference, carelessness and neglect. Persons can be indifferent to entities only because we can care about them whereas a door, for example, is neither concerned with nor indifferent about anything. Being is not an issue for doors. The process of there-being, however, is always occupied with and by the entities that it encounters in the world - caring or indifferent about things and loving, hating or indifferent about other human beings.

The Founding Mode of Being-in-the-world. The observation that being a person is necessarily a being-in-the-world breaks with the traditional notion of your being in the world as a subject among objects who best 'knows' the world reflectively by 'standing back' and thinking about it 'objectively'. Being-in-the-world is more like being in love - loving another is not a matter of knowing what love is but of engaging in a certain way over time with certain possibilities presented to you by the world. As a person, you are not primarily a spectator/knower but an actor/participant. You first

21

understand the Being of entities in the world by using them; you then want to know about them in order to use them better and/or more fully. Humans will have discovered the categorial properties of various trees, for example, by using parts of trees to serve their existence - making fire, weapons, shelters, medicines, dyes, and so on. This is why being-in-the-world comes before understanding which, in turn, comes before theoretical knowledge.

Following the traditional subject/object dichotomy, one of the most common philosophical pictures of personhood is that of a thing-like mind, soul, or essence that has beliefs about the world. In this picture, knowing about the world is foundational to being a person. The big issue for such an entity is that it is trapped inside a body and/or consciousness and can never know for sure that the objective world [seen as the collection of things outside of the person's mind] is as it seems to be. If Heidegger's observations are right, however, *the founding issue for being a person is that of choosing what kind of existence to live and, thereby, what kind of person to be*. You want to know stuff only because, and in so far as, it matters to this. If you want to be [exist as] a hunter then you need to know about the location and vulnerability of game animals, if you want to exist as [be] a gardener then you need to know what plants will grow in your environment and how to grow them successfully. Being a hunter, gardener, neither, or both, are possibilities for existing. Having to choose an existence is why you Care. Knowledge arises from [is founded on] caring about your existence, so knowledge about the world is not your founding mode of being a person in the world - Care is.

2.1 Being-in-The-World

Although being-in-the-world is primordially and constantly a whole, we can ask three different questions of it: we can ask *what* being-in-the-world is, *who* is being-in-the-world and *how* that entity is being-in-the-world. These three are considered respectively in chapters 2.1, 2.2 and 2.3 (always keeping in mind that asking different questions of the same being-in-the-world does not imply that being-in-the-world has three aspects or parts).

If you assume that a person is basically some kind of mind, soul or consciousness, then you are going to begin any inquiry into being a person by considering this mind or whatever. Only then would you move on to how it relates to the world. If, however, you understand existence as *essentially* a matter of being-in-the-world then you are going to include the nature of the world into your analysis of being-in-the-world right from the beginning.

Being-in-the-world as a person discloses that the world in which you exist is not just a bunch of things in space but as a working environment for existing in one way or another. The feature of the world, which enables it to play this role in your existence, is its worldhood. **Worldhood** is a complex integrity of roles, concepts, projects, functions and functional interrelations, that arises from, and serves, various possibilities for existing in different ways. The worldhood of a teaching environment, for example, is not desks and so on but a rule-governed complex of ways in which persons, tasks, furniture, buildings, books, and such like, are related to each other around certain ways of existing.

The worldhood of the world is what makes the things around us cohere as a meaningful integrity [a world]. It is also what allows and invites us to encounter objects in the world as variously meaningful or not. To get the worldhood of the world into view, Heidegger considers everyday interactions, with entities in the world, that casts an existential light on its own environment. Our use of utensils (doorknobs, plates, hammers, etc) is just such an interaction.

In the everyday process of being-in-the-world, you encounter the objects in your environment as variously relevant or irrelevant to your chosen existence. These - called 'ready-to-hand' and 'present-at-hand' respectively - are two basic categories of Being for the objects that you encounter in the world.[5] Things **present-at-hand** are in the world but of no immediate relevance to what you are doing. **Ready-to-hand** things, events, persons, and situations, on the other hand, are relevant to your existence either as a help or as a hindrance (e.g., any given climate, for example, is ready-to-hand as conducive to certain ways of life and as inimical to others).[6]

---

5. A third basic category is other persons, who are neither present-at-hand nor ready-to-hand but encountered as 'being like me'.

6. Traditionally, humans have tended to consider the Being of all entities, including themselves, as present-at-hand. This is misleading because Being is meaningful, the meaning of Being is existential, and the existential Being [meaningful character] of entities is disclosed

Ready-to-hand objects can be assets or liabilities. Heidegger calls the ready-to-hand assets 'equipment' to highlight the fact that their Being is that of tools and/or resources for serving a possible existence. Wind, for instance, becomes equipment when we use it for windmills, yachting, flying kites, paragliding, and so on. **Equipment** [a ready-to-hand asset] includes anything that is assigned a purpose - e.g., schools [equipment for teaching and learning], rooms or houses [equipment for residing], water [equipment for irrigation, swimming in, travelling on, generating electricity], and so on. The Being of equipment is defined by the practices in which it is employed, and its properties are established in relation to the norms of those practices. The Being of ready-to-hand areas of land, for example, emerges from their being actual or possible equipment for playing games, farming, building, photographing, making a nature reserve, and so on.

Items of equipment are always used **in-order-to** achieve some purpose which serves an existence; parking spaces, for example, are created in order to park vehicles, and make sense only within a **totality of equipment** [all the ready-to-hand assets in the world]; a parking space is only a parking space in relation to a totality of vehicles, roads, places of work, shopping regions, and so on. Because equipment is always used in-order-to do something, there are a multitude of

---

only when they are ready-to-hand for a mode of existence and meaningful for this reason. You cannot, for example, disclose the *Being* of an earthquake until you grasp its place and function in the existences of persons being-in-the-world.

existence-generated relations which define its place within both the total sum of equipment and the practices of its employment. These relations all begin and end with a person or persons using equipment for existing in one way or another. As we have seen above, the worldhood of a teaching environment consists of a set of meaningful relationships between various equipment and the existences of various persons. Likewise, the worldhood of the world generally is made up of an interrelated web of assignments and references, that is; a set of towards-which (below) relationships between items of equipment and various persons (the **reference**) and person-related in-order-to tasks (the **assignment**), within which the items have meaning. To disclose the Being of a school, for instance, you need to know the tasks to which it has been or can be assigned, the materials it works with, and the existence-serving projects in which it is or can be used. The assignment gives the in-order-to Being of the school, the reference gives you its **for-the-sake-of** Being; the school is, in other words, usable in-order-to teach and learn for-the-sake-of teachers, learners and their community. It is the in-order-to and for-sake-of-which that you understand (qv) when you disclose the Being of the school.

The relationships, which make up the worldhood of anything (including the world itself) are meaningful by being '**towards-which**' relations in which each 'node' of assignment and reference web 'points' towards another node. A school desk, for instance, indicates processes of design, manufacture and transport - each of which is towards-which other activities (mining metals, producing wood and plastics, energy systems, and so on).

The towards-which relations of equipment derive from the being-towards of the persons who use equipment in the service of their existence. **Being-towards** is a constant and essential aspect of being-in-the-world whereby persons are always oriented towards various objects of attention that are of concern to their existence. If you desire chocolate, for instance, then you are being-towards chocolate; if you are resisting that desire then there will be 'counter-weight' being-towards of some kind (being-towards losing weight, reducing acne, managing your sugar levels or some such). There-being is always being-towards comprehendingly - i.e., unlike things, persons variously understand or misunderstand what their existence is being-towards.

The relevance of entities in the world depends on your existence; the behaviour of fish, for example, is relevant to fishers in a way that it isn't to farmers. It follows from this that you tend to be-in-the-world on the lookout for entities that are relevant to your existence; you are, in other words, being-in-the-world on the lookout for possible equipment. This 'being on the lookout' for equipment is **circumspection**. If, for example, you are a fisher or a farmer then your awareness of the weather is circumspective - you are sensitive to changes in the weather that serve or threaten [have meaning for] your chosen existence. Circumspection is the perceptual framework you get when you have a need or project in mind; it is not disinterested and not contemplative. This is because circumspection goes with Care as a way of discovering objects that are ready-to-hand as a possible resource or asset. It is because you are being-in-the-world circumspectively that you tend *not* to pay attention to entities that are merely present-at-hand (i.e., not relevant as possibilities for your existence).

The alternative way of paying attention to entities - **reflection** - is a deficient (qv) mode of circumspection in which you disengage yourself from being-in the world; you, in effect, 'stand back' and consider objects of attention as present-at-hand ('objectively'). The difference being circumspection and reflection matters because circumspection discloses the Being of entities but reflection does not. Reflection doesn't disclose the *Being* of equipment because their Being is in their involvement in existence, and this Being is not disclosed when you consider phenomena out of their existential context. If, for example, if you use a brush for painting then that use discloses its Being [its meaningful character as equipment]. But if you reflect on the brush when it is not being used for any existence-related purpose then its Being is obscured [closed off]. Circumspection discloses a brush as variously serviceable or unserviceable to your existence; you sight it as handy for painting, dusting, cleaning your teeth, or whatever. Contemplative reflection, however, sees the brush as bristles and a handle. That can be handy if you want to make or repair a brush but it is not the same as disclosing what it is when it is being a brush (i.e., it does not disclose its Being as a brush).

Use of the words 'sight' and 'seeing' here is deliberate because while we sense ['see'] numerous phenomena everyday, only sight is a matter of seeing something as ready-to-hand. **Sight**, which is a metaphor for all circumspective awareness (smell, touch, hearing and so on), is meaningful seeing through being informed by worldhood. The worldhood of the world makes circumspection possible; you couldn't be-in-the-world on the lookout for resources [equipment] unless you were already embedded as a potential equipment-user in a worldhood of equipment use whereby equipment was understood as relevant to various forms of existence. Circumspection, in turn, makes sight possible by disposing us to be aware of objects as possible equipment. Sight, in other words, is '*seeing as*' - e.g., being aware of the weather as a possible asset or threat to your existence.

You can explore the worldhood of equipment by tracing its towards-which (assignment and reference) relations. Say, for example, that you start with a pair of shoes. You can trace the worldhood of the shoes back through their sale, distribution, design and manufacture to farming for leather and cotton, mining and smelting as a source of metal for the needles that sewed them together, oil refining as a source of glues, plastics and paints, and so on. At all points of this journey you disclose not only ready-to-hand things and their context but the existences of persons who use them (and, of course, the making of shoes in the first place is only something people do because we have uses for various kind of footwear according to their chosen existence). Thus it is that, through these referential relations, the public world pervades every use of equipment.[7]

The Being of equipment is normally inconspicuous. If you are using a brush to paint with, for instance, you tend to ignore the Being of the brush and simply use it to get on with the painting. You normally notice the Being of handy objects only when they become 'unhandy' in some way (e.g., the brush breaks, gets clogged or worn or whatever). If this happens, and the brush is considered reflectively, it becomes deprived of its worldhood so that its being ready-to-hand is lost (i.e., the ready-to-hand becomes unready-to-hand). This means that we tend to notice the Being of equipment only after it is made conspicuous by *not* being what it usually is (as when, for example, you suddenly notice a paint brush that won't paint because it become clogged with dried paint), doing this brings out the character of equipment as unready-to-hand, and that,

---

7. Some folk equate the world with nature. But it is only through the existences of persons that the world of nature is discovered and **'environed'** [made part of the larger world]. Persons disclose the sky as beautiful, for example, only if disclosing beauty is part of who they are choosing to be. While many things are present-at-hand prior to being ready-to-hand (bauxite, for instance, was a part of nature for untold millennia before persons discovered the smelting of bauxite into aluminium),it is the handiness of ready-to-hand things that provides their ontological [meaningful] Being. So what makes your sight of a desk, for example - that which reveals its Being as a desk - is not its material constitution but its place in the overall scheme of things to do with persons being-in-the-world. This is why the mere aggregation of plants, animals, rocks, water, etc, is not enough to make nature a world.

in turn, explains why persons tend to confuse the world brought to our attention in this way - a world in which we are spectators rather than actors - as what the world 'is'.

Heidegger interrogates being-in-the-world because this activity discloses Being. The problem is that we tend not to disclose Being in our everyday existence, and the normal alternative [reflection] doesn't disclose it authentically. If you tend to notice the Being of objects only in a reflective state, when they are detached from their everyday Being, then what you think that you have disclosed is not, in fact, the authentic Being of the object (disclosing a brush as bristles and a handle is not the same as disclosing its Being as equipment for painting). If you notice the Being of entities in your daily world only when they are not being used towards some end (e.g., when they break and/or when you reflect on them), then you not only lose sight of their Being but also of your Being as a person who uses equipment for-the-sake-of an existence by which you realise yourself as one kind of person or another. It's almost as if you start making yourself a function of worldly facts (a thing) instead of deliberately choosing an existence because it realises the kind of person you want to be.

As we have seen, equipment is encountered within the world as a 'workshop' of being a person. The relationship between the world and a piece of equipment is such that the world must already be at least implicitly understood as a workshop before you can disclose the Being of equipment. No one, for example, discloses a hammer as equipment for hammering unless she has some notion of hammering and how it fits into the larger scheme of things (i.e., the worldhood of the world). So the environmental context [the worldhood of the world], in effect, **frees** the Being of items to be disclosed. This is possible only because persons themselves set up the totality of assignments and references within which things can be ready-to-hand in the first place. The world, as a meaningful environment of existence, is our creation. The hammering ability of a hammer, for example, is not a property of the hammer in the way of its colour, shape or mass. Anything ready-to-hand is simply appropriate [serviceable] for some projects and inappropriate [unserviceable] for others; and its 'properties' as something ready-to-hand are bound up in the ways in which it is appropriate (which is why a hammer-shaped polystyrene stage prop is not an authentic hammer even if it is the right shape and size, and has a perfect wood-and-steel finish applied to it). For something to be appropriate for a purpose, it must have been assigned a purpose. And to say that the Being of equipment has a 'structure' of assignment or reference entails it having been assigned to some purpose by some person; assignment is a function of a person or persons making or adopting something for-the-sake-of an existence. Assignment, therefore, entails involvement in some person-relevant project, and the character of Being which belongs to equipment is just such an involvement. An **involvement** is a matter of being engaged in or with something to do with the existences of persons - and it is the 'in or with' relationship that is invoked by the terms 'assignment' and 'reference' (in-order-to and for-the-sake-of). When someone or something is involved in or with something, then that person or thing has been assigned to a role in some

32

activity with which it is involved. A hammer, for example, becomes equipment for hammering by being assigned to the role of hammering. I am a hammerer by assigning myself to the role of using a hammer. Such assignment requires some person to do the assigning and some human project in which the person and hammer are involved (e.g., the building or repairing which makes hammers meaningful entities and is referenced to a person or persons whose existence is served by the building or repair).[8]

The assigning of things to purposes is something that you do constantly and, in doing this, you assign *yourself* to a role within the context or frame of reference [an integrity of assignments and references] within which things in the world are ready-to-hand. This is also something which you do before you use an implement or space for an assigned purpose. Using a brush as equipment for painting, for instance, requires your prior Being as a potential painter. The 'context of assigned relations' is the world, and the locating of ourselves within the world - giving ourselves a place within the context of assigned relations involving implements, purpose and persons - is the 'worldhood' of being-in-the-world persons just as it is the worldhood of things.

---

8. As with the term 'existence', involvement has a meaning that is referenced to being-in-the-world. A snail's shell, for instance, is not involved with safely or shelter in the way of human houses or clothing because the snail is not a person who has assigned its shell to the task of realising one possible existence rather than another.

On the basis of the foregoing analysis it can be seen that:

- The worldhood of equipment is what ready-to-hand assets are in terms of their assignments (in-order-to) and references (for-the-sake-of).

- The worldhood of the world is the condition which makes it possible for us to discover and disclose things as equipment within the world. This disclosure provides a way of figuring out the being-in-the-world of persons.

- The worldhood of persons is their being within the world as the assigners of equipment, themselves and other persons to various projects which have meaning in reference to a possible existence.

- One way of putting this is to say that the worldhood of the world is the integrity of everything within the horizon of significance. An **horizon** is any finite framework within which certain entities are being what they are and/or various activities take place. **Significance** is the relevance that various equipment has for different kinds of existence. The significance of equipment is constituted by relationships of towards-this, in-order-to (assignment) and for-the-sake-of (the reference). The world itself is disclosed [revealed as a world] by the significance of its contents. It is the totality of significance which constitutes the understandability [intelligibility, qv] of the world.

Spatiality. Things in the world are in space and time, but being-in-the-world is spatial and temporal. Categorially, space and time are relationships.[9] Spatiality and temporality, however, are ways that there-being orders equipment into 'beside, above, behind' relationships, and being-in-the-world into 'before, during, after' relationships. Although categorial concepts of 'being in space' and 'being in time' dominate our interpretation of being-in-the-world, only existential analysis can disclose the Being of being in space or time while categorial [reflective] analysis closes it off.

Spatiality is the aspect of being-in-the-world whereby persons arrange the 'workshop' of there-being according to the relevance that various entities have for our existence. A cook in a kitchen for example, does not relate to entities in the work space in terms of mathematical coordinates. The space is arranged, rather, in terms of cooking equipment being clustered beside, above, below, on top of or behind other equipment according to its relevance for the work being done in the space - preparation surface here, heat source there, frequently used preparation equipment closer to the preparation surface than less used items, and so on. As a person, the world is a workplace and your being-in space is that of a worker being-in a workspace. Like the cook in a kitchen, persons arrange and experience the space of the world in practical terms according to which items are used for what projects; medical equipment is clustered around patients and medical staff in hospitals, religious equipment around

---

9. Although some physicists treat them as honorary things of obscure thingishness.

ministers and worshippers in churches and temples, domestic equipment in homes, and so on.

To someone measuring distances and angles between objects in a kitchen, all space is equal; all centimetres, for example, are the same length and the observer is equally detached [remote] from the objects being located in mathematical space. To a cook preparing food in a kitchen, however, the meaning [Being] of spatial relationships is measured in terms of relevance and convenience - he or she wants equipment within easy reach.

Categorially, you are closer to what is at hand than you are to objects more distant. The role of relevance and convenience in spatiality, however, entails that you are *existentiality* close to what concerns you and remote from what doesn't concern you. If you are standing on one side of a crowded street, for example, a friend or enemy that you see on the other side of the street will be existentially closer to you than the strangers who are categorially close. As most objects in the world are not of immediate concern to us, remoteness is the normal state of everyday spatiality and has to be overcome when you bring objects of concern into a close relationship.

Remoteness is your normal spatial relationship with objects in the world in which you are detached ['severed'] from them by their irrelevance to your existence (i.e., you *see* numerous entities but *sight* very few). Remoteness [being 'severed' from the Being of what is before and around you] is a default position which you have to overcome by de-severance (qv).

The contrary to remoteness is closeness. **Closeness** is an achievement in which you bring what is normally remote close to you by your concern. So, like all aspects of lived [existential] spatiality, closeness is measured in terms of relevance rather than yards or metres. When you perceive the world circumspectively, things that are relevant to whatever project or projects motivates your circumspection will tend to be closer to you - they 'leap out' - than will things that are irrelevant even if those irrelevant things are categorially nearer. That is why sighting your lover across a crowded space brings her closer to you than people you don't care about who are actually touching you as they pass. This closeness is achieved by the way that Care de-severs you from the normal remoteness of objects.

Persons arrange the world spatially by being-in-the-world as workers in a workshop. Our arrangement of space creates places. A **place** is where sets of related equipment belong in the arrangement of your working environment. The place for kitchen utensils, for example, is in a kitchen. Having a place is different from being at certain navigational coordinates because it has to do with equipment having a function. The place of the controls of a machine, for instance, is where the person using the machine can readily get at them. If an item doesn't have a place in the scheme of things then its position is just a 'random occurring', a 'lying around' as something present-at-hand.

All places are part of a 'zone of operations' or 'whereabouts' ['whither'] assigned to a related set of activities - e.g., kitchens, workplaces, homes, schools, or marketplaces. Spatially, these areas of your environment are **regions**. The existential spatiality of a region is made up of the use which makes it relevant to you, and its direction and range relative to where you are. So regions make up the wider existential (existence-related) spatiality of the world around us. If you work in a hospital kitchen, for example, your 'here' [where you are] is defined by you in terms of distance [range] and direction to the places assigned to various functions within the hospital as a region of health care (e.g., wards, reception areas, theatres, consulting rooms, imaging suites and so on).

When it comes to locating yourself in an environment, you do not rely on some kind of internal gyroscopic compass but on your relationship to objects in that space; you are 'on the Third Floor by the lifts' or 'on my way home from school' or 'at the bus stop', and so on. These relational items (3rd Floor, school, bus stop) are the '**yonder**' from which you *derive* your '**here**.' This is because your being-in-the-world is in the *world*. Within this world, the yonder is all the things around you, having a place in a region, by which you locate your 'here' as a worker in the 'workshop' of the world. Your spatiality, as a worker being-in a workshop, is lived in terms of your distance and direction from various objects of concern of your chosen work [existence]. These objects are the 'landmarks' of the 'yonder' from which you derive your 'here.' This is why, if you think "Where am I?" you immediately think of yourself as located among things in the world. If your being-in-space was internal then you would always know where you are; you don't always know where you are, and when you are lost it's

38

because you cannot locate your 'here' to a meaningful 'yonder' - you don't recognise this road or those houses. It follows from the nature of being-in-the-world that yonder is the actual 'dwelling place' of there-being as Care because you live your life as a person engaged with various objects of attention that are relevant to your existence (you do not live in your head or heart or mind or whatever, but in the world). Yonder is where you are being when you are there-being.

2.2 Being-One's-Self

If you ask *what* being-in-the-world is then the answer is "The activities described in 2.1". If you ask *who* is being-in-the-world then the answer will be an individual "I am". This 'I' who is being-in-the-world is your Self.

Like so much else about being a person, the Self is normally considered in thingish terms as a soul, ego, personality, consciousness or whatever. Your personality and history, however, are just aspects of your facticity; as potentiality-for-being your **Self** is no-thing but the connection by which you are the same 'I' over time and change. Science defines the way that actualities remain as what they are over time and change in terms of substance (i.e., how the stuff they are made of is arranged and coheres), but the way that a potentiality remains as what it is over time and change is by maintaining itself as the same potentiality over time. Being the same Self over time and change is not based on the substantiality of a substance but on the *'s elf-subsistence'* of an existing [living] Self. Where substance is thingish (the word 'substance' is a noun) **self-**

subsistence is an *activity* undertaken by an entity that maintains itself as itself in a world and over time. As potentiality-for-being your self is *characterised* by your personality and history but cannot itself be reduced to either.

If you want to disclose your *Being* as a Self then it is important not to confuse the 'I' who is maintaining itself as itself over time with the kind of self-thing that seems evident to reflective attention. The reflected-on self-thing is a bunch of bodily, ethical and psychological characteristics which change dramatically over time. You Self is what remains the same despite those changes. No quorum of bodily, psychological, historical, 'spiritual' or other such characteristics disclose the Being of your Self - only a relatedness which ties your entire existence together *over time* can do that. So the reflected-on self, the self-thing of tradition, is a false representation of the existential self.

Having to maintain yourself as the same Self over time and change (i.e., from being a tiny baby through adulthood to old age) is an important reason why your being your Self is temporal (i.e., holds the past, present and future together as a single 'horizon' of existence).

Being-one's-self [being-a-self or being-your-self] is a life-long everyday activity which each Self must undertake for itself. However, although every Self is being itself for itself, it does so in an essentially public world. You do not, for example, invent being-in-the-world for yourself but learn it from others. This has a profound effect on how you are being-your-self because the language, beliefs and biases of your community shape the way that you exist even when you are on your own. This means that being-one's-self unavoidably includes certain social structures of being-with other persons in some sort of community.

Being-with is the fact that being-one's-self always and *essentially* entails the influence of other persons. There is nothing optional about being-with, and it is not simply a matter of sharing a world with other persons because having a world in which to be a person wouldn't be possible in the first place except in natural/cultural environment that persons share with each other. Being beside, being alone, being away from, or being missing, are all derived from being-with. The only reason that you can feel alone, for example, is because being-with others is primordial and being alone is a deficient [derived] mode of being-with. If being a person is essentially being-with then the influence of other persons is an essential facet of being-one's-self. This inescapable integrity between being-one's-self and being-with others is a major influence on your existence.

Others are beings who are not us but are like us in • being neither ready-to-hand nor present-at-hand • being-in-the-world and • (in our particular case) being human. Just as there-being is never without a world so is it never without others. The encounter with other persons is quite different from our encounter with things; we do not, for example, encounter human-like shop mannequins in the way that we encounter

41

humans. This means that we are not just being with or not being with other persons; we are being-with them.

Being-with is the fact that existing [being-in-the-world as a person] is always, necessarily and inescapably bound-up with the existences of other persons (there-being is *essentially* being-with). For persons, being with other persons is being-with others in much the same way being in the world is being-in-the-world.

The influence that others have on you is that of what Heidegger calls 'they'. The **'they'** is not a particular set of people so much as a set of communal values to which groups of persons conform (and usually without even noticing that they are doing so). 'They' are peer pressure, the shared assumptions of a language, historical conventions, the social norm or 'done way of doing things' which determines your existence. The 'they' are everywhere and nowhere, and we are all members of 'they'. The 'they' is not the 'them' of an 'us or them' dichotomy but the 'us'; it is the abstract 'everyone' of "Everyone knows..." acting as an influence.

The important facts about the 'they' are that (1) it is a communal influence rather than any actual group of persons, and (2) you *are* influenced by it. So the 'they' is a kind of mutual cultural coercion.

As you are busy about your everyday life and being-with 'they', so the 'distances' between yourself and others diminish. Social **distantiality** has to do with how closely you fit into a 'they.' It is measured by any differences between yourself and 'they' which inhibit your acceptance by your cultural community (e.g., your family, neighbours, age group, co-religionists, peers, or whoever). Distantiality is why you feel uncomfortable wearing out-of-fashion clothes or not thinking, talking and acting like others; not liking or disliking what 'everyone' does.

Issues of distantiality arise because, and disclose the fact that, being-one's-self stands in subjection to 'they'. If you are going to get by in the everyday world then you need to fit in, to be respected if not liked. Doing this involves **averageness**; that is, a way of being-one's-self in which your existence becomes pretty-much interchangeable with that of other folk in your community. The more Hindu you are, for instance, the more your existence is interchangeable with every other Hindu. The same goes for being a teacher, a farm worker, a doctor, or a soccer hooligan. This is an unsettled [**turbulent**] existence because the internal politics, fashions, loyalties and jargon of any group is constantly changing. Being-with 'they' is a matter of being constantly driven by the ever-changing currents of group dynamics; of always having to be-with what or who is in or out of favour.

Regardless of which community you are being-with, or how determined you are to own your own existence, you will end up conforming with a communal paradigm of how to exist. This conformity homogenises ['levels'] your possibilities are 'down' to a norm. **Levelling** is a kind of homogenisation that goes with fitting in. It is usually a matter of levelling off or levelling down because levelling tends towards averageness.

An important feature of all the above is that the 'they' is a communal coercion which you internalise from infancy so that what you think of as your 'privateness' is mostly a 'publicness.' **Publicness** is internalised averageness; an unknowingly self-inflicted conformity and levelling down which dominates your existence. It is the set of 'normal' assumptions, beliefs and attitudes which dictates the process of being-one's-self in ways, and to an extent of which, folk are normally unaware (and certainly underestimate). It is the way that the 'they' world infects your personal being-a-self. When you engage with the world, you do so in terms of internalised public assumptions - you take it for granted that the world, truth, goodness, success, gender and so on, are as you are conditioned to believe by 'they'. Publicness thus rules not only on what you consider is right and wrong, real and unreal, but also what you are and what is possible for you.

Being-with 'they' matters to Heidegger because publicness obscures the personal existentiality of being-in-the-world which, if not obscured, would disclose the there-being that discloses the meaning of Being.

Publicness is pervasive ['alongside everywhere']; we are born into it and seldom even notice it unless conscience (qv) bothers us. One reason for this is the way that being-with 'they' disburdens us of the bother for being-a-self for ourselves. Through publicness, the inconvenience of being-one's-self is given away to your daily round and/or membership of some community. Moreover, just by doing this in publicness the 'they' creates its own invisibility; the 'they' is not something you can take a hold of, it is just 'how things are'.

Publicness informs your being-one's-self to such an extent that the normal human person is a **they-self**; that is, a self that maintains itself by being absorbed in everyday life and believing 'they'. The they-self is still being-in-the-world but does not own its existence in an understanding of what it is to be-in-the-world authentically. We are all normally a they-self simply because we are and have to be-with the 'they' just to get along as persons in the world. You did not start out as authentic self and then 'lose' yourself in publicness; you started in publicness - being a they-self is normal and primary. This means that being-one's-self is **lost** in being a they-self. This lostness explains why, even though there-being as a person necessitates disclosing Being, the normal human being-a-self fails to disclose the existential Being that Heidegger is after; we have covered up our Being as potentiality in everydayness.

Your 'lostness' in the 'they' is not a matter of having displaced your 'real self' in the way you might displace an item of clothing. So disclosing authentic being-in-the-world is not a matter of seeking out a certain kind of primitive character. Disclosing the authentic Being of persons, would be a matter of 'clearing-away of concealments and obscurities, a breaking up of the disguises with which There-being bars its own way'.

2.3 Being-in-the-World

We now know what being-in-the-world is, and who is being-in-the-world, analysing how we are being-in-the-world brings us to the 'there' of there-being. The '**there**' of there-being is *not* a geographical location (not a 'here' or 'yonder') but the disclosive nature of being-in-the-world. The process of being a potentiality in-the-world over time necessarily discloses the Being of • phenomena [objects in the world], • the world itself and • being-in-the-world - not just as what they *are* but, more importantly, as what they *mean* to those who exist as persons by being-in-the-world. Persons disclose the Being of their personal [existentiell] being-in-the-world by their moods, their understanding, and discourse [talking about the world and being-in it]. These could together disclose the true Being of existence, the world and objects in it, were it not that our normal mode of being-in-the-world is lost and fallen (qv) into the world of 'they'.

Disclosure (1): States of Mind. Moods disclose how you have so far experienced having to be-in-the-world as you and it are. All sorts of emotions may come and go during a day. But, underlying these, there is a more basic and enduring **state of mind** which is a kind of overall 'emotional attunement' to being-in-the-world as you have so far found it. Your state of mind looks back to the past and discloses the way that you feel about having found yourself 'thrown' into the world as what and who you are. As such, your emotional state of mind discloses your being-in-the-world as a matter of concern to you. That is why persons, and only persons, are assailed by moods; moods are an existentiale and persons are never free of them; even apathy and indifference are moods.

Thrownness is the fact of finding yourself landed with the task of being someone you didn't choose to be in a geographical, social, and historical, world that you didn't choose to be-in. What you are thrown into is your facticity (qv) both as inherited and as chosen. Whether you are born rich or poor, black or white, tall or short, male or female, you must realise your possibilities as the person you find yourself being and in the world as it is.

Heidegger's metaphors of finding yourself 'thrown' into a world and 'delivered over' to yourself, are not intended to suggest that some purposeful force or agency has placed you as what you are into a time and place; they just capture the fact that, as a person, you 'awoke' to personhood to find yourself already landed with being a particular person in a particular environment. You have to live with being this person at this time and place; you are the person that you are, at the time and place you are, whether you like it or not. Your mood discloses the Being of this 'having to' as you have experienced it so far.

Thrownness is not a 'once for all time' event but an ongoing fact of your existence; you are always being-your-self on the basis of a facticity with which you are landed. If, for example, you are disabled in an accident then you will have to cope with that disability as part of the world into which you find yourself thrown. Whenever you make a choice, having to live with the

47

consequences of that choice becomes a part of your thrownness as soon as the choice is made. Obligations, debts, good luck, and bad choices that you are living with now, are the most obvious examples of this fact.

Being thrown into this world, as what, where, when and who you are, is not something that you can 'get behind' and change. The victim of an accident cannot, for example, go back to before the accident and avoid having been disabled.

The fact of having to be a particular individual, in a particular world, matters to you. There have been possibilities for pleasure and pain, success and failure, in the world; there have been choices to make without knowing enough to be certain that you are choosing well; there have been resources you didn't have and resources that you had but wasted or were not sure what to do with. The Being of all these past facts is disclosed by the mood [your attunement to having-being-in-the-world] which discloses your state-of-mind. In disclosing the Being of your having-been-in-the-world, your moods bring you before yourself. Given the chance, you may well have preferred a more congenial being-in-the-world. You may have preferred having being born in a different place or time, to have had and/or made different choices in your life, to have a different body, or even not to have been a person at all. The fact is, however, that you find yourself 'thrown' into the task of being who you are in the world as you find it - and the Being of that task so far is what is disclosed by your state of mind.

Your state of mind discloses the Being of your thrownness in two basic kinds of mood: those in which you emotionally 'turn towards' a fact, and those in which you emotionally 'turn away' from it. Turning away discloses your thrown Situation (qv) by trying to disavow some aspect of it in some way. If you turn away from a fact of your past or present existence, for example, then you disclose it as distasteful, embarrassing, and/or a threat to who you are trying to be.

You are always in some sort of state-of-mind because you always have some sort of attitude towards the facts of finding yourself thrown. You may be powerless to go back and prevent an accident, for example, but you still have to take some sort of attitude to it. This attitude discloses how you have been coping with it so far. You might have a seriously uncongenial being-in-the-world, and you might hate having been landed with it, but wishing won't make it go away; you have to exploit or neglect your possibilities as who, what, and how, you are, not as who or what you'd prefer to be. And, in having a mood, you disclose yourself as someone who has been 'delivered over' to a circumstance as who you have to be. Most human persons, in fact, turn away from the reality of being thrown and, in doing this, further obscure their true, existential, Being.

Disclosure (2): Understanding. Whereas mood discloses the being-towards-the-past aspect of your being-in-the-world, understanding discloses the being-towards-the-future aspect.

Understanding is your immediate and practical disclosure of objects as possible equipment for existing in one way or another. If, for example, you can use a desk in-order-to actualise a possibility, for-the-sake-of your existence, then you understand it's being a desk. As such, understanding does not require that you be able to spell-out the desk's construction, history or material constitution; it is enough that you can use it. To do this requires some kind of general pre-conception of possibility. With the reference to possibilities we get to the being-towards-the-future aspects of understanding. Persons disclose the possibilities of things because the possibilities of things derives from the possibilities [potentiality-for-being] of persons - we understand the possibilities of fire, for instance, by projecting our potentiality for being fire-users onto it. This, in turn, discloses at least some understanding of our own being-towards the future.

There-being is a **potentiality-for-being** which always has more than one possible existence before it that it could choose. You always have, for example, the potentiality-to-be a gambler by choosing a gambler's existence, the possibility to be loving by choosing a loving existence, and so on. As with possibilities, your potentiality-for-being is limited but real. It is because of your potentiality for existing in one way of another that Being is an issue for you, you Care, you have to be engaged with a world, and you integrate the past and the future in your present being-in-the-world. Potentiality-for-being contrasts with **facticity** - which is your actuality as an already-defined being; facticity derives from the past while potentiality is being-towards the future. Potentiality-for-being is a primordial and defining feature of being-in-the-world a person, and is the reason why there-being is always more than its present facticity.

Possibilities are not a product of things in the world but of the integrity of being-in and the-world. This is because the possibilities of things, which your potentiality-for-being discloses, are themselves a product of your potentiality; rocks are possible tools or weapons only because persons are potential builders and fighters.

When you understand something in terms of its possibilities for serving or hindering your existence, you do so by 'projecting' your potentiality-for-being onto them. **Projection** could be likened to throwing 'the light of understanding' into an obscure area in order to bring certain possibilities to light (as when we talk about someone 'throwing some light on the subject'). It is, for example, projecting your potentiality for being a learner that leads you to understand certain states-of-affairs as possibilities for learning. Because possibilities become actualities only after the moment in which they are disclosed as possibilities, projection is always being-towards the future. Understanding is projective because you can grasp an object's possibilities only by imagining a future that is different from the present; that is, by projecting your disclosive there-being forward into futures where various possibilities are or are not actualised.

This why it is understanding that discloses the being-towards-the-future Being of being-in-the-world. If you lived entirely in

51

the present then you could not even understand any object of attention as a possibility let alone act on it. Understanding wheat as possible flour, and flour as possible bread, for instance, needs the existence of a person [a potentiality-for-being] to see beyond what presently is to what possibly could be (i.e., to project beyond the present and into the future). Just by being a person, you understand entities in the world in terms of possibilities even if you don't spell out that understanding to yourself.

As a person, you are yourself 'thrown' into being-projective. This means that you have no choice about being projective; it is part of being a person. Being ahead of yourself, by acting for the sake of your future self, is an activity which you cannot avoid. So projection is not a matter of something that you do only when you think of it or are planning a big project; being projective is what you are as a potentiality-for-being who deals with actualities in terms of their possibilities.

As with every other aspect of being-in-the-world, understanding can not only be variously accurate or mistaken but also authentic or inauthentic. Authentic understanding would not lose sight of the process whereby the possibilities presented by objects of attention has its Being through the projection of your potentiality-for-being.

Interpretation. Understanding not only discloses possibilities but has possibilities of its own. One of these is interpretation. **Interpretation** is a slight extension of understanding by which you work out the possibilities projected in understanding. If you *use* a door in-order-to access a place then you understand it, if you *sight* it as a door (as being in-order-to control access to places) then you interpret it. This interpretation has an '...as...' structure; you interpret what you use 'as' ready-to-hand. In the normal course of events, circumspection sights entities both understandingly and interpretatively.

Interpretation matters only because it is, in effect, a step away from practical understanding and towards an intellectual [thematic] articulation of an object's character. It precedes any judgement as to an object's serviceability, usability or detrimentality because you have to have some idea of what an object is for (its in-order-to) before you can judge how useful or not it is for the job. But if you continue this development, begun with interpretation, then the next step is articulation - which takes you away from understanding, which discloses Being, and towards reflecting on an entity as present-at-hand, which closes Being off. **Articulation**, as a development of interpretation, is the literal or metaphorical/intellectual dis-integrating of a complex integrity into the linked parts from which it is constituted. So say, for example, that a device you normally use stops working. If you examine the device's components to find the problem then you are articulating it (i.e., tracing how all the bits fit together). Once you can follow how a bit fits and is involved with other bits as part of an entity, then you grasp the bit's meaning.

Meaning is where and how a component of a component of a larger integrity (a device, a region, the world) fits within the articulation of whatever integrity of involvements it plays a role. The meaning of a word, for example, is how it fits into the world of language (i.e., the task to which it is assigned in a language). The meaning of an event is where it fits into the world of events. The articulation of meaning is finally a matter of placing things into the wider context of the world [the whole natural-social environment within which things have possibilities]. This is why things and events can be meaningful only as part of a world.

If an object can be fitted into an integrity of involvements then it has meaning; if it cannot then it is meaningless. The meaning of a door, for instance, is what it is used for in projects that serve the existence of persons in one way or another. Things in the world don't somehow have a meaning in the way that they have an internal structure which can be discovered by dissecting them.[10] Meaning is a matter of persons making

---

10. Neither the world nor objects in it are intrinsically meaningful or meaningless because meaning is an existentiale of there-being - not a property attaching to entities. Animals that are not there-being do not, and cannot, take hold of their own Being in an understanding of possibilities. Crabs, for example did, do not 'give up their forelegs' in order to evolve claws as part of being one kind of crab or another, and their having claws is not meaningful to them. The meaning of crabs having claws is available only to persons because only persons can *interpret* crabs' claws as a kind of tool that serves the crab (i.e, interpreting the claws of a crab as equipment by falsely projecting the Being of person into them). Persons can interpret crabs in this way only because persons alone are a potentiality-for-being for whom the way that things fit or don't fit with each other is of vital importance in the project of self-making in, and by means of, the world. This is why there are no secret meanings hidden behind appearances. For anything to have a meaning it must have been

sense of the world by tracing the assignments and references which give the world its worldhood. It is that articulation that makes the world intelligible. **Intelligibility** [understandability] is the totality of assignments and references by which you make sense of things (i.e., interpret them in the light of assignments and references which give them their meaning in terms of persons being-in-the-world). As with meaning, intelligibility is not a function of things but of persons projecting their own potentiality-for-being onto things.

Although the process from understanding to intelligibility seems straightforward, to articulate [spell out] the meaning or intelligibility of objects (a ladder, for instance) you must already have an interpretive fore-structure - a frame of reference into which you can fit your articulation of the assignments and references by which a door and its components gets their meaning as part of a whole. All interpretation works from a fore-structure, so where understanding looks forwards, interpretation and articulation look backwards to a pre-existing [historical] fore-structure. We are, in other words, slipping from circumspection into reflection.

Assertion. You can understand, interpret, and articulate, an object without saying a word. But, more often, you do 'say a

---

assigned a role by a person. The occult meanings supposedly disclosed by superstitious folk are not assigned by planetary or other arrangements but by those who seek to make themselves significant in this way.

word' by making assertions such as "This bit goes here and connects to that thing." An **assertion** is a proposition, that is, a particular use of language in which you say [assert] something about something; a pointing out which discloses and communicates a definite character which something has. The proposition "This bit goes here" is an assertion; it predicates a fact ("...goes here") about a subject ("This bit...").

Assertions are often taken as the paradigm of language use when they are, in fact, grounded in discourse (qv) - of which they are just one kind. By asserting that an object has a particular property, you lose sight of the larger [existential] context which alone discloses the object's Being. Where an articulated object has its Being in relation to existence [being-in-the-world], its properties have their Being in relation to the object; asserting that the object has a property narrows your focus from the object's Being to 'this bit here.' This changes your relationship with the object by detaching it from its Being in the worldly environment and focussing only on the question of whether or not it has a certain occurrent [present-at-hand] property.

What we have here is a continuation of the process by which the Being of objects, which is disclosed by use but made inconspicuous by familiarity, is slowly being hidden by the very process by which we think that we are making their Being conspicuous. Assertions obscure the ready-to-handness of objects and replaces it with a kind of present-at-handness. This obscurity isn't 'bad' - so long as it is understood - but it can be misleading if you come to believe that you are disclosing the Being of an object when you can articulate the physics of its structure when, in fact, its Being is not disclosed by its physical constitution but by its use in various projects that serve various modes of existence. You do not disclose the Being of a desk by taking it apart and/or listing its physical properties; you disclose its Being by noticing how you use it. The same goes for the there-being of persons which Heidegger wants to disclose. He cannot disclose the Being of persons by interpreting and/or articulating them biologically, psychologically or anthropologically; there-being is *existence* [being-in-the-world] and must be disclosed existentially.

Disclosure (3): Discourse. **Discourse** is a matter of persons communicating with each other verbally, pictorially, by gestures or in writing, as a way of disclosing their own Being and the Being of entities which they encounter in the world.[11] Its most fundamental mode is ordinary face-to-face discussion and it has always been the primary way in which persons disclose and communicate the Being of things to each other, especially in the sense of bringing the attention of others to what is there but has been hitherto unnoticed. As we have seen, assertions alone can be misleading because they close off the totality of involvements that discloses the Being of objects. Discourse achieves a more authentic disclosure by expressing the intelligibility of things - their meaningfulness. It does not create or 'call into being' the things, events, and

---

11. This is why hearing and keeping silent are both modes of discourse. You can, for example, disclose Being by not saying anything - especially when other folk are talking idly (see *reticence*).

activities, which it makes manifest. Talking of imaginary objects such as Taniwha or the Earth Goddess will not bring them into existence because discourse is just talk, it has no magic powers. However, discourse can bring ephemeral situations into focus in a way that nothing else can. For example, a person who is troubled by a problem is often advised to 'get it out into the open' by talking about it. The insight justifying this advice is that discourse discloses states of affairs - it makes them manifest - and so presents them as objects of attention which can be dealt with straightforwardly as objects rather than as abstractions or chaos.

Language - the totality of signs, figures of speech and rules of grammar - is the equipment that you use for discourse. But it is discourse [the project], rather than language [equipment], that provides the framework with which you need to be familiar in order for language to make sense. You could not, for example, ask "What is love?" unless you already understood the public ritual of question and answer. Once again, however, you must be careful not to let this fact drive a wedge between you and the world. Although your understanding of word use can come only from a prior acquaintance with discourse (which is a public phenomenon requiring a world in which other entities are being persons), the disclosedness of discourse is integrated with the world. Love, for instance, is a possible mode of existence and, for discourse about love to disclose the Being of that mode, the discourse must be integrated with it in some way.[12]

Discourse discloses your being-in-the-world just as much as do states of mind and understanding. Moreover, in your discourse, you disclose your understanding and your mood. So discourse, mood and understanding are three internally integrated aspects of your existential constitution as a person - three equally fundamental aspects of your being disclosive.

Since your being-in-the-world is being-with (qv), discourse is being-with others as a medium of communication and communion. The problem with discourse, when it comes to disclosing the thrown and projective Being of being-in-the-world, is that, by being 'fallen' into idle talk, curiosity and ambiguity, our everyday discourse doesn't disclose our true Being so much as obscure it [close it off].

2.4 Fallenness

In your average everyday mode of being a person you maintain yourself as a they-self (qv). So articulating average everydayness entails asking how the they-self exists - a task which also entails asking why humans are normally so

---

12. Heidegger himself does not investigate the integrity of discourse with existence. The most plausible analysis, at the moment, is that of Ludwig Wittgenstein in his *Philosophical Investigations* (first and standard English translation, by G. E. M. Anscombe, published by Blackwell, Oxford, in 1953).

unaware of their own Being. Heidegger answers this last question in terms of idle talk, curiosity, ambiguity, and falling. Putting it briefly, what happens is that, in our everyday being-with each other, our discourse becomes dis-integrated from the Being that it purports to disclose - it becomes 'idle'. This disintegration leads to curiosity, in the form of seeking for novelty, and an ambiguity whereby you no longer distinguish truth from what is merely engaging and/or fashionable. All of these together help to institutionalise a fallenness in which we lose sight of our Being.[13]

Idle Talk. Talking and writing isn't all about making true or false assertions about the world. As a disclosure of Being, however, discourse integrates what is said with an object of concern in a world.[14] In **idle talk**, what is said overcomes our concern for the object in such a way that we take what is said for granted, allowing it to 'infect' our understanding of the subject; we then accept and pass on what is said as true. In this process, we think that we are learning something about objects in the world at the very same time as we are actually losing touch with them. By losing touch with the supposed

---

13. The failure of fallen everydayness, to disclose the Being of there-being, is the reason why Heidegger devotes so much of *Being and Time* to working out what unfallen [authentic] there-being would be like.

14. One of the ways in which we interpret love, for example, is in fiction (literature and drama), poetry and music. Indeed, fiction, simile and metaphor interpret love more persistently than do our scientific, pseudo-scientific (psychological, sociological) or phenomenological analyses.

objects of our talk, what we hear and say becomes groundless and, by mistakenly thinking that we are gaining in understanding, we close off not only the objects of our talk but also the possibilities of further discovery about them. So if, for instance, folk in your everyday world talk about ethnicity as determinative to character-definition then you will begin to interpret human Being just as if ethnicity mattered in the way 'they' say it does. Consequently, a kind of pseudo-disclosure of Being - the 'received wisdom' of the 'they' - comes to dominate your being-in-the-world (in the case of ethnicity, as an often violent barrier to relationship).

Discourse is engaged with Being. Idle talk is idle by being disengaged; it has a life of its own that, in effect, floats on top of the world. Although popular nature or history documentaries are more insidious modes of idle talk, the kind of celebrity gossip found in certain magazines and newspapers is probably the most obvious mode. In idle talk you receive, discuss and pass on, what is said without checking the veracity of the claims. Idle talk takes on a life of its own which becomes increasingly detached from what it is supposed to be about. The claims of such talk then become the interpretations and half-truths which 'everyone knows' as you are 'delivered over' to them. Most of what you hear, say, read, watch on television or write in your lifetime is idle talk or **'scribbling'** [the written mode of idle talk, found mostly in newspapers, magazines, 'self help' books, and popularisations of science, religion, and so on]. This kind of verbal activity doesn't disclose being-in-the-world so much as close it off with assumptions, half-truths, unsubstantiated claims, gossip, and conventional prejudice. The irony of this is that we take idle talk as teaching us something about being-in-the-world at the very same time as we are actually losing touch with it. This doesn't just counterfeit the disclosedness of discourse, it perverts the very act of disclosing into an act of closing off because what is said in idle talk is understood as disclosing something. By losing touch with Being, what we believe becomes groundless (qv). And, by mistakenly thinking that we are gaining in understanding, we close off the possibilities of authentic disclosure.

Idle talk and scribbling express a kind of thinking that goes with average everydayness. The 'average intelligibility' of 'they' pronounces on everything and is the authority whose interpretations become the whole justification for what you believe. And the they-self doesn't distinguish this authoritative pseudo-justification from real disclosedness. Indeed, one reason that idle talk appeals to humans is that its very groundlessness presents us with a supposed possibility of understanding everything without having to go to the bother of checking it for ourselves - we are 'spoon fed' intellectual junk food, rather than harvesting truth for ourselves, because it is fast, tasty and easy to digest.

All human understanding, interpreting and communicating flows out of and back into the 'average intelligibility' established by idle talk. This is not an alien environment, it is your 'home' which you carry with you like a snail carries its shell. Idle talk is not deliberately or maliciously misleading, nevertheless it is mischievous because it permeates your entire understanding of what it is to be a person. The pseudo-disclosure instituted by idle talk and scribbling entails that unlearning what you have supposedly learned from them becomes necessary for any attempt at truly disclosing Being. This is far from easy.

Curiosity [novelty-seeking]. The pseudo-disclosure of truth in idle talk has been 'uprooted' (i.e., it is no longer integrated with the Being it purports to disclose), so what you have in average intelligibility is a kind of free-floating mythos that feeds on itself rather than on any actual Situation. It is, moreover, this mythos rather than the world which we take as authoritative. Perhaps even more to the point, this cultural 'junk food' feeds us as well in the sense that we maintain ourselves with idle talk in our average everyday lives. So instead of authentically being-in-the-world, we merely 'float' alongside it - being tethered to average intelligibility by its apparent omniscience, confidence and the security of what 'everyone knows'. Moreover, and because we are so used to our tether, being without it feels unnatural (un-home-like or 'uncanny', qv).

By being detached from the true disclosure of Being, the pseudo-disclosure of idle talk tends to drift away from what is actually there in the world and towards the exotic, alien and remote. Our discourse seeks new objects of concern not in-order-to grasp in their Being but in-order-to stimulate our interest. In short, we become novelty-seeking. Curiosity is ordinarily a normal and important part of your being a person in the world. Being-in-the-world is primarily a function of concern which expresses itself in circumspection. Idle talk, however, detaches us, and our curiosity, from the world - our concern is no longer for being-in-the-world but diversions from being-in-the-world.

Novelty-seeking [**curiosity**] is the restless [turbulent, qv] search for new objects of interest as a distraction from the burden of authentically being-in-the-world for ourselves. It comes into play when your interests become detached from being-in-the-world and attached instead to idle talk. As your curiosity becomes detached from the true, existential, disclosure of being-in-the-world so you become increasingly distracted by new possibilities; you seek the novel in worlds that are different to your thrown environment. As this happens you linger in any given 'world' for shorter and shorter periods of time and, by drifting everywhere, you 'dwell' nowhere. This is perhaps best seen in the way that persons are taken by the novel in dress, religion, entertainment (including travel), diet, self-understanding or ideology. To such persons - i.e., all of us to a greater or lesser extent - what is sought is distraction; we are actually fleeing the burden of being-in-the-world rather than authentically realising our potentiality-for-being within it. As is so often the case with half-truths, we usually mistake this restlessness for being open-minded and/or full of life.

Ambiguity. Idle talk and curiosity inform and motivate each other. And the blend of the two, with its allure of supposedly unlimited personhood, is profoundly seductive. But, perhaps more importantly, by being systematically detached from the true disclosure of being-in-the-world by idle talk, we lose the important ability to distinguish genuine disclosedness from its counterfeit. This **ambiguity** is a condition in which truth, half-truth and untruth become so mixed that you cannot pick your way between them. Everyday ambiguity comes about because idle talk is more attached to what 'they' say than the actual world, and the authority of the 'they' carries more weight with us than does your own intelligence and understanding. So when, for example, books like *The Last Cabbalist in Lisbon* or *The Da Vinci Code* come along, purporting to be historically disclosive, then the very people who are sceptical of the historical eyewitness accounts that they have of the events in question will accept as reliable the misrepresentations of a highly biassed novelist some centuries removed from those events.

The inherent ambiguity of idle talk is allied to everyday curiosity in a manner shown by the way in which complicated and/or 'mystical' pseudo-disclosure is, and always has been, routinely acclaimed as 'deep and meaningful' while real understanding is dismissed as dull and boring. The world of idle talk is the 'wide and easy way' that leads to being closed off from our own Being. But in a public world, dominated by idle talk and curiosity, ambiguity permeates the very understanding into which all of us find ourselves thrown as part of your inheritance as persons. You are thus fallen into an already existing inertia, a 'current' against which you must 'swim' if you are to disclose being-in-the-world to yourself.

Fallenness. Being a person [there-being] is always somebody's **'mine'** as we each live our own lives for ourselves. However, although we are each living our own lives and cannot do otherwise, we normally lose the personal ownership of our own existence by being absorbed in an habitual daily round and following a communally-defined way of life. The problem with this is that it gives a false [inauthentic] picture of existence which obscures the 'mineness' of there-being.

There is no ethical implication to the term **'inauthentic'** - no suggestion that the inauthentic life is somehow inferior to an authentic one. *All* existence is fundamentally 'inauthentic' [un-owner-like] because it is inevitably defined to a great extent by the culture, society, and everydayness within which it is lived. The only issue with existing 'inauthentically' [within a community], as we all do, it that it obscures the personal aspects of there-being that Heidegger seeks.

Fallenness is the normal (inauthentic) mode of everyday existence in which persons fall into the everyday world and being-with others to the extent that we no longer sight (qv) of our being-in-the-world as potentiality-for-being. Like the term 'inauthenticity' the term 'fallen' is not pejorative; it has no religious, moral or political overtones. The term is simply used to signify the normal 'being caught up in the everyday world' that obscures the disclosedness of being-in-the-world (the 'there' of there-being) which Heidegger wants to interrogate.

By being fallen into [caught up in] the everyday world you are fallen away from being-in-the-world for yourself. Because everydayness constitutes the dominant and normal mode of your existence, you mistake the kind of they-self that you are in the world for what you really are (i.e., thrown and projective).

Fallenness is the mode of being a person into which you were born and within which you live your everyday life. In this mode you are cut off from authentic concern for the world, and authentic solicitude for your fellow humans, by your absorption in everyday existence. Because your Being as a person is one of being-in-the-world, this dislocation entails that you are cut off from an authentic understanding of yourself [your Being as a person]. This explains why human persons, to whom an understanding of Being belongs, nevertheless cherish social, religious, philosophical and scientific traditions which systematically misrepresent the existence of persons by interpreting our Being in a way more fitting for things. Our inherent sociability, and subsequent tendency to lose ourselves in the 'they', means that ambiguous they-truths become embedded in the idle talk from which our religious, philosophical and scientific 'experts' take their cue. Because experts are held in high esteem, this pseudo-expertise then gains the over-inflated authority of what 'they' know. Moreover, our curiosity means that the only challenge to this comes from trendy ideologues and pseudo-philosophers who offer novel theories which basically assault commonsense with complicated and/or mischievous nonsense. None of this is accidental because falling is built into our social absorption into the 'they' and thereby into being the they-self that we normally are. This being the case, falling is not just an historical fact of human personhood but a definite existential characteristic of there-being itself.

Humans persons wouldn't be universally fallen unless there was something in it for us. We are all tempted by fallenness, and no one is tempted by any possibilities for being a person unless they are already being-towards the kind of person for whom the possibilities in question are relevant. To be tempted to steal, for example, you must already be covetous. This is why any possibility by which you are tempted discloses something about who you are choosing to be. In this case, the relevant possibility is very evidently an escape from the bother of being-in-the-world for ourselves - aided and abetted by being-with 'they'. Being-with 'they' is an unavoidable aspect of your everyday life that contains within it the possibility of fallenness which is tempting to those who want to flee from the burden of having to be a person. So **temptation** - our willingness to flee from the burden of personhood - is the ground of fallenness that is itself prepared by idle talk and the way things have been publicly interpreted by 'they.'

Fallenness is tempting, in good part, because authentic being-in-the-world entails anxiety (qv) and the average intelligibility of being-fallen 'tranquillises' us. **Tranquillising** is the way in which our being-with 'they' replaces anxiety with confidence. 'They' know everything; if a problem threatens then 'they' will come up with some solution - all we have to do is wait for 'they' to work it out and tell us what it is. When you buy into this, as we all do to some extent, then you 'tranquillise' yourself into thinking that anxiety is unwarranted. Being is no longer an issue for you; you become confident that 'everyone knows' that the values of your 'they' are all there is to it.

This is not a serene state so much as a stupefied one, and, ironically, tranquillising your being-in-the-world finds expression in busyness. Tranquillising typically expresses Care in the form of a 'make work' in which folk attend, often quite minutely, to the tasks and rituals of everyday life - doing the job, saying the prayers, attending meetings, classes or seminars, chanting mantras, keeping up with the latest news, going to the café or pub, and so on.

Keeping busy alienates you from being who you are for yourself. With further irony, this self-alienation often expresses itself in self-entanglement. In **self-entanglement** you picture your Being as thingish and try to figure out the thing you supposedly are in order to disclose its Being. Becoming fascinated with 'discovering' ourselves is a perennially popular diversion from the inconvenience and uncertainty of having to be-in-the-world as a potentiality. Instead of understanding our character as an ongoing artifact of a chosen existence, we treat our character as the artifact of some external force or agent - God, evolution, economics, planetary alignment, genetics [nature] and/or upbringing [nurture], karma, the 'masters of the universe' or whatever. By alienating us from the bother of being-one's-self, fallenness attracts us to a kind of exaggerated self-dissection, tempting us with every sort of they-explanation - scientific, religious, psychological, astrological, Druidic, Freudian, Marxist, ancient Egyptian, and so on - until you are swamped with a whole array of 'characterologies and typologies' purporting to disclose what you are. In this kind of self-entanglement we seek to understand ourselves, and others, as a 'that' - a woman, a social product or personality type, a Maori, a sports fan, a Sagittarian, a teenager, a Christian, a Canadian, and so on. This, once again, disburdens you from the bother and anxiety attendant upon having to create and maintain a character for yourself.

2.5 Care

What we have considered so far are the many aspects of everyday being-in-the-world. This kind of existence obscures whatever it is that makes all of these aspects meaningful; the question is, "Why do persons exist as they do". Answering this question will be a matter of 'looking through' all the multiple activities of there-being, which cover it up, to sight a 'unitary phenomenon' which explains all of them. This integrating factor is Care (qv) - a phenomenon which announces itself in the form of anxiety.

Anxiety is not the fear of something in the world (such as an upcoming exam or confrontation), but the uneasiness or dread which accompanies having to choose a possible existence at the expense of others (which might be more valuable if you only knew it). You normally spend your life fleeing anxiety, and experience it only if your everyday existence breaks down and confronts you with the need to choose a new way of being-in-the-world. What is particularly scary, and revealing, about this anxiety is its disclosedness that being-in-the-world stands on *potentiality* rather than being a thing. All moods and emotions have an emotional object. The emotional object of anxiety, that before-which you are anxious, is the fact that (a) you have to choose an existence for yourself by actualising some possibilities at the expense of others, and (b) the world of possibilities, by which you choose a possible existence, is itself a product of the existence you choose (it is only the potentiality of there-being to exist as a builder, for example, that discloses the possibilities for building, in the world, that are valuable to the person who is being a builder). There is, therefore, no final foundation to being-in-the-world, no actuality which determines your values.

Anxiety is the primordial and authentic mood of persons[15] in which you confront the very Being from which you have turned away in falling - a being defined by possibilities [states of affairs which, just by not yet being, are no-thing]. There is nothing irrational or unjustified about anxiety even though, when you escape it, you agree with those who deceive

---

15. Keep in mind here the difference between being a human and being a person. It is only for human *persons* - animals for whom possibilities are objects of understanding - that anxiety is primordial and authentic. Other animals may experience fear or stress that is analogous with ours - even though we do not and cannot know what other animals are experiencing - but they could be anxious only to the extent that they are being persons because only persons have to choose an existence from possibilities that are disclosed as possibilities only by being-in-the-world as a potentiality.

themselves that it is silly, foolish or pathological. Nevertheless, anxiety makes you feel not only scared and insecure but also insignificant. Indeed, falling into the everyday world is tempting precisely as a means of fleeing anxiety.

Anxiety throws you back on your own potentiality-for-being. It discloses that nothing makes you into a teacher or builder or Presbyterian; nothing will even make you go on surviving if you choose not to. In everydayness you hide your Being in being-with, but anxiety individualises you. **Individualisation** is the disclosure of your mineness (qv) as a potentiality-for-being who has to choose the existence that will disclose possibilities that being-in-the-world has for you. To say that anxiety individualises you is not to say that it strips away your public mask and reveals some sort of 'essential personality'. This cannot be the case because your moral and psychological character is and always has been continually defined and redefined by your ongoing existence. Anxiety individualises you not as a specific actuality but as a specific potentiality (a 'no thing') that has to define an actual character *for itself* by existing in one way or another. This calls you to make up your mind ['take a stand' or be resolute, qv] about how *you* are going to exist rather than drifting along in everydayness.

By disclosing being a person as what it truly is, anxiety discloses that, contrary to the sense of belonging which you assiduously cultivate in everyday life, you are not really 'at home' in the world. Heidegger calls the disturbing feeling of not being 'at home' in the world being 'unheimlich' ['un-home-like'] The German unheimlich is usually translated as 'spooky' or 'eerie' but is rendered as 'uncanniness' in the best extant English translation of *Being and Time*. **Uncanniness** describes how being-in-the-world feels to us when stripped of its comfortable and familiar covering. Being a they-self makes us feel 'at home' in the world - a feeling apparently validated by the tranquillising confidence of idle talk. You are encouraged, by your acceptance by 'they', to feel comfortable with being a they-self in a they-world. Anxiety, however, jerks us out of our absorption; the world no longer feels comfortably familiar, our tranquillisation fails.

Care as the Ground of Anxiety. You experience anxiety to the extent that you Care and, as well as individualising you, anxiety discloses your Being as Care. As we have already seen, **Care** is the existentiale by which facts, possibilities, people and events in the world variously matter to you in one way or another. Care is enacted in and as all the aspects of there-being which we have looked at so far. It is, for example, Care which explains both moods and understanding because if you didn't care then you wouldn't be affected by the world and wouldn't be motivated to understand it. Care also explains the difference between things ready-to-hand (those that immediately matter to us) and present-at-hand (those that do not immediately matter to us). Care explains your interest in other folk and what they do (solicitude) and your concern for states of affairs in your environment. Indeed, every aspect of there-being hitherto encountered 'grows' from Care.

How you care or don't care now always has elements of the past and future in it; what you do now depends on who you have been up until now and who you intend being after now. This is the temporal [time-relevant] structure of Care; the Being of there-being is Care and Care always integrates who you have been and who you will be with who you are being. So understanding the temporality of Care is essential to understanding the Being of there-being.

Care has three temporal aspects (the '**Care structure**'). Who you have been as Care (thrownness) is being-already-in (qv), who you will be as Care (projection) is being-ahead (qv), and who you are being as Care (fallenness) is being-alongside (qv). This three-part structure comes about because, for persons, caring in the present is always bound up with caring about the past and future. The tripartite temporal structure of Care is **primordial** to being a person because there is nothing under, behind or more primitive than Care when it comes to explaining the meaning of why persons exist as the do. If anxiety discloses your Being as Care, and Care is inescapably temporal ('stretched across the future, past, and present') then anxiety shows you the essential temporality of being a person.

Although Heidegger doesn't get around to disclosing the Being of temporality for a little while yet, it pays to be aware that, as with spatiality (2.1), temporality is an aspect of being-in-the-world; we do not discover time by being born into it but categorise events in time by being temporal. **Temporality** is an existential phenomenon whereby being-in-the-world as Care requires (**a**) ordering existence into 'has been', 'is being' and 'will be', and (**b**) holding the past and future *together* in the present. Categorial measures of time are public equipment, derived from our temporality, that help us to do this.

The temporal structure of Care matches the temporal structure of your there-being as mood, understanding and fallenness. Your mood is being-towards having been thrown into being-in-the-world as inherited from the past. Understanding is being-towards the future as projective. While fallenness is being-towards the everyday present. The simultaneity of these is shown in existence. Say, for instance, that you are facing a risk and decide to take it while being careful. In such a case you are acting in the present, as who you have been so far, and for the sake of who you will be after the careful risk has been taken. If you decided not to take the risk, or to take it carelessly, then you would create a different character for yourself by how you act [exist]. In such cases, however, you would still be acting now, as who you have been, for the sake of one of the potential characters you can be. Thus it is that your Being as Care not only encompasses being-alongside [in the midst of] the world in the present but also being-already-in the world [having a past] and being-ahead-of-yourself [having a future].

As thrown projection, you are an integrity of actuality (the thrown) and potentiality (the projective). This integrity is temporal because who you are in the present is defined by who you have been in the past while you project your potentiality into a future by your present choices. Your being-in-the-world is always being-towards the future by 'reaching' towards being someone who you are not yet (but will be with any sort of luck). However, this **'being-ahead-of-yourself'** is integrated with your thrownness - your already being-in a world - which is why Heidegger talks of there-being as 'thrown' projection. It is only within the integrity of the actual and the possible (i.e., yourself as both thrown and projected) that your 'being-already-in' in effect buries your 'being-ahead' (your potentiality-for-being) in the world. Thus, fallenness is the mode of there-being into which you 'flee' from the anxiety of being-ahead. This, in turn, is the very mode from which you can find yourself (reluctantly) freed by anxiety.

There-being, Disclosedness and Truth. Being-in-the-world as Care discloses the significance of the world, its components and being-in-the-world. This disclosure is capable of being more or less true. The common notion of truth is of an agreement between an assertion and what the assertion is about. The problem here is how you could know that words and objects agree unless you already knew the truth about the object? You can, for example, adjudge the assertion "Radiata pine is a fast growing softwood" to be true only if you know that radiata pine - the thing itself - is in fact a fast growing softwood. This, however, suggests that truth is not in the relationship between words and objects but in your original disclosing of the objects themselves. The true disclosure of Being is primary, the truth of assertion derives from that. **Truth**, therefore, must be a kind of 'uncovering', a disclosure, of states of affairs that is prior to the truth of assertions.

Truth, in this sense, is a disclosure of Being and untruth is an obscuring [covering] of Being.

Getting at the truth (i.e., disclosing the Being of entities) is part of being a person in the world because it is a function of concern which, in turn, is a function of Care. If folk didn't care about the possibility of harvesting timber, for instance, then the Being of radiata pine as a fast growing softwood would never have been disclosed. This means that truth, in the 'truth as uncovering' sense, is a function of there-being - which is itself being in the truth just by doing what it has to do to be-in-the-world. That aspect of there-being whereby you cover, uncover, discover or are mistaken about, the Being of entities, is your being in the truth. **Being in the truth** does not mean that whatever you believe is true but only that the disclosure of truth is an essential aspect of there-being. A tree, for example, cannot have false beliefs about itself or the world because it cannot have true beliefs about itself and the world. Persons, on the other hand, can have true or false beliefs about themselves, the world and each other. So we now have three aspects of truth:

- The being in the truth of persons being-in-the-world;
- The truth of entities disclosed by persons being in the truth; and
- The truth of propositions, as an agreement between entities and what is asserted about them.

The whole of truth cannot be reduced to the truth of propositions because propositional truth is the aspect of discourse that derives from the truth [disclosedness] that emerges from persons being in the world by being-in-the-world as Care.

Some people talk as if truth was some sort of thing-like essence that exists independently of us; some kind of meta-narrative 'lurking' in worlds or states of affairs which you may or may not discover. This is not so. There is no Truth with a capital 'T' somehow hanging around 'out there' - there are only states of affairs which have meaning to the beings whose potentiality-for-being gives them meaning and whose being-in-the-world discloses it more or less accurately. It is only being-in-the-world that makes truth possible and talk of truth meaningful.

This does not mean that, under dichotomy, states of affairs only recently disclosed were somehow false before they were 'made true' by being disclosed. All it means is that, before discovery, such states of affairs were neither true nor false because truth and untruth come into play only when the Being of an entity is disclosed by an entity that is being in the truth. There may be eternal or absolute truths but, because truth is relative to persons in worlds, such truths would require eternal or absolute persons in eternal and absolute worlds (although I am not sure what an 'absolute' world would be). The fact that truth is relative to there-being, however, does not mean that truth is relative in the sense of "It's true if it's true to you". Truth is disclosure, and what is true is what is disclosed in the *world* - not what you would like to believe has been disclosed. There is, in other words, 'a truth of the matter' that depends on us to disclose it.

3. Being-a-Whole, Being-Towards-Death

The existence that has been described so far does not disclose the whole of being a person in the world. It seems obvious, for example, that Heidegger cannot describe the whole Being of a person without including the role of death somewhere in his description. The problem here, however, is that, although death ends being-in-the-world, there is no time, alive or dead, when a person is actually whole or complete. Your there-being is one of potentiality; you are therefore necessarily incomplete for as long as you live and any possibilities at all remain open to you. However, coming to an end of your possibilities at death doesn't complete you; it merely brings your potentiality-for-being to an end. This being the case, death doesn't seem to give a whole picture of being a person so much as simply stop there-being from ever being whole. So, if you are going to account for the role of death in there-being, you are going to have to look at the role it plays in your existence before you die (your **being-towards-death** as the way in which your existence is affected by being thrown into finitude).[16]

---

16. Appeal to a supposed afterlife may postpone this dilemma but does not actually resolve anything because, for as long as you are a person, in any world whatsoever, you must have possibilities - that is simply what it is to be a person. This means that your self will not be complete. If this state of affairs ever ends in any way whatsoever (e.g., after several lives, or by your selfhood or consciousness being absorbed back into the 'great ocean of being,' or whatever) then you will no longer be a person. This means that, even if there was an afterlife or lives (which is unlikely) there would still be no possibility of anyone narrating an existentiell experience of themselves as a whole because there will never be a time when the person is both

Categorially, what death is or isn't is moot. Existentially, however, **death** is the end of the individual's potentiality for being one kind of person or another by being-in-the-world. Death, in this sense [the end of *existence*], typically coincides with **perishing** [the end of biological life] but, for the purposes of getting the existential meaning of death into view, these need to be distinguished. Thus, just as many beings live but only persons exist as well as living, so we can say that all living things perish but only persons die as well as perishing.

What matters for disclosing the whole of there-being is the meaning of death. Being-with-others is part of being-in-the-world, and it is from the deaths of others that most of us take our understanding of death. However, even being alongside the dead in mourning and remembrance cannot really disclose the true existential meaning of death because it is not your being-in-the-world that has come to an end in these cases. Just as existence is always someone's 'mine', so too is death - only the individual person can die her own death just as only she can live her own life. This means that the meaning of death cannot be grasped via the deaths of others. To disclose the true Being of death for an individual existence you must focus on what the death of that existence means to the person whose existence it is.

---

complete and still existing as a person.

    * If you find yourself harbouring a belief that some religious or metaphysical narrative offers a way out of this dilemma then, for the sake of your own understanding, you should assume that you haven't fully grasped the significance of the issue.

Part of the meaning of death, for persons, is that, for us, death **impends** [looms over our lives] in a way that it doesn't for other living beings. Death impends for persons because we do not know when or how we are going to die but we do know (a) that we will die, (b) we could die at any moment, and (c) our death will be the end of our potentiality-for-being in this world. So for persons, to whom life is the ever-present possibility of possibilities, death impends as the ever-present possibility of impossibility.

Death does not merely impend in the way of a coming storm or visit to the dentist. This is because these events are part of being-in-the-world and being-with others which you will outlive. Your death, however, is something 'distinctively' impending because, unlike other impending events, it is that possibility which is:

- Your **ownmost**. Like your pain, your death is yours and yours alone. Another can give his or her life for you, but no one can die your death for you any more than you can avoid dying at all.
- **Non-relational**. The world and the 'they' of social Being are made irrelevant by death. When you stand before your own death, all your relations to other persons are undone.
- **Not to be outstripped**. There is no 'getting around' death, no outrunning it. Death strips us of all our possibilities but is itself the one inevitably possibility of which we are not stripped by anything.

These, together, constitute the existential Being of death. And authentic or inauthentic being-towards-death, as impending, your ownmost, non-relational and not to be outstripped, needs to be included in any true disclosedness of being-in-the-world as a whole.

The non-relational aspect of death is such that, in authentic being-towards-death, you stand before your ownmost potentiality-for-being; the esteem of others, and what they expect of you, is irrelevant. Moreover, being-towards the ever-present possibility of impossibility dramatically highlights your being-towards all your existential possibilities. In other words, an authentic being-towards-death provokes an authentic being-towards existence.

Being thrown into death is part of being thrown into **finitude**, that is; the limits to your possibilities arising from (a) your mortality, (b) your circumstances, (c) what you are [a particular human being], (d) the nature of world in which you exist, and (e) the fact that actualising some possibilities entails not being able to actualise others. These limits are variously logical, physical, psychological and temporal; you cannot, for example, escape being-towards death, the 'laws' of logic or nature, your physical limitations or your social-historical thrownness. Despite this, your attitude towards the end of your possibilities - your being-towards-death - can be variously authentic or inauthentic and is usually the latter as you 'flee' from the meaning of death just as you flee from your existence as a person.[17]

Being-towards death as a 'someday' actuality or gateway into another existence is inauthentic by turning away from the meaning of your death for your being-in-the-world (i.e., the meaning of death as the ever-present possibility of impossibility).

Our normal, inauthentic, being-towards-death is, like our average everyday being-towards life, basically one of evasion, concealment and idle talk. We act as if only other people die, we 'console' the dying with lies and euphemisms, death is sanitised with talk of sleep or life after death. This is all part of being a they-self in which 'they' provide tranquillisation about death. This public tranquillity is shown in the way that death is so often seen more as a kind of social inconvenience, a nuisance, rather than the uttermost end of potentiality.

In the 'they', we hide from the responsibility of being-in-the-world as potentiality and Care; it requires no courage to be part of the 'they', there is no anxiety because the 'they' has everything under control. But 'they' are also a kind of oppression that doesn't allow authentic being-towards-death.

---

17. Persons do not, for the most part, have any explicit knowledge that they are delivered over to death, or that death thus belongs to being-in-the-world. Thrownness into death sometimes reveals itself to persons as anxiety. Anxiety in the face of death is not the same as fear of death but is an awareness of that we have only a limited time to be who we are.

Authenticity is suppressed so that the cultivation of a supposed indifference to death alienates us from our ownmost, non-relational, potentiality-for-being - we do not face death, which requires courage, but turn our faces away from it. This evasion of death is inauthentic.

Although Heidegger didn't have access to a community of authentically existing humans, his analysis of the Being of death enabled him to give an informed projection of what an authentic being-towards-death would probably be like. Death is, for example, absolutely certain. The certainty of death is not the kind that you get through the gathering of evidence. It is of a more primordial kind than intellectual certainty because it is part of your existential certainty of being-in-the-world. The point here is that your existential certainty of death, like your existential certainty of life, and unlike your theoretical certainty of death, is not inductive ("Everyone dies, I am part of everyone, therefore I too will die"). It is more that you know that your possibilities are limited because it is possibilities that you live by; there is, if you like, a primordial understanding of death as finitude 'built into' your being a potentiality. It is only when you are certain then you act with conviction. **Conviction** is a form of certainty in which you let the truth be the sole determinant of your being-towards it understandingly. If this is right then authentic being-towards-death would act with conviction in life; death wouldn't be abstracted from life but faced as what it is as part of life.

The end of your potentiality-for-being, although certain, is uncertain with regards to its certainty because you never know when you will die. This uncertainty is disclosed in anxiety, and only if you are willing to pay the price of living with your anxiety can you achieve the authentic being-towards-death which provokes an authentic existence. This is because the anticipation of death individualises you as already shown above; to be individualised just is to face the fact that you, and you alone, realise your own potentiality in your own way and in a manner for which only you can be responsible. It is facing this reality, this responsibility for your own values and meaning, that the anticipation of death can free you for.

Heidegger's initial description of authentic being-towards-death is couched in negative terms - it would not evade reality, would not cover it up, and so on. But if everyday being-towards-death is inauthentic because it flees anxiety, etc., then he can start working out what an authentic attitude might be like from what the inauthentic attitude is not. Taking this approach discloses a distinction between awaiting death, which is normal, and anticipating it.

Anticipation is a response to being thrown into death, as the final end to our potentiality, in which we accept death as impending, our ownmost, non-relational and not to be outstripped. We can get a sense of what Heidegger is getting at with anticipation if we think of the way that some folk keep themselves ready to seize certain opportunities when they arise and/or make the most of their fleeting opportunities while they exist. So, far from making life pointless, authentic being-towards-death offers support for becoming intent on something. The anticipation of death 'switches on' your ownmost potentiality-for-being; it provides the impetus for living life authentically. Anticipating death entails projecting yourself upon your present possibilities (i.e., the only ones that are actually open to you). One of the ways in which it does this is by 'wrenching' your existence away from the 'they'. Your death has nothing to do with the 'they' - it is yours and yours alone.

The anticipation of death does not mean 'waiting for' or 'dwelling on' it but understanding that you are finite - particularly in your possibilities and the time you have to realise them - and existing as an authentic person in the face of that (there is no truth-denial, responsibility-denial, or wishful thinking in anticipation). So anticipation of death would be part of being-in-the-world authentically.

3.1 Potentiality-for-Being Authentic, Resoluteness

To ground his projection of authentic being-in-the-world would be like, Heidegger requires some empirical evidence that will **attest** to [provide evidence for] our potentiality-for-being-authentic. This evidence is found in the fact that only persons have a **conscience**; that is, an awareness of responsibility.

Persons have an awareness of responsibility, and this awareness [conscience] seems to be common to all human cultures even though the laws and values of those cultures varies considerably. Moreover, conscience is always experienced as a personal call to individual responsibility, and if the call is not acted on then it has to be suppressed. Being a 'call' makes conscience a form of discourse. Discourse is always addressed by someone to someone and always has a subject [that which is talked about]. In the case of conscience the someone it addresses is the individual, and its subject is something about the individual's personal being-in-the-world. In doing this, conscience calls individual there-being to awareness of its own Being as Care. What conscience tries to tell the individual is usually suppressed and/or clouded by excuses, publicness and/or popular mythology. But, if you look past the local details and towards what your own experiences of conscience have in common, you may notice that your conscience is experienced as a kind of call that summons you to be responsible for some aspect of your own existence.

To speak of conscience as a 'call' implies the existence of a caller - the 'someone' who is addressing you. The call of conscience originates within you, but the caller is obviously not who you are as a they-self; after all, conscience 'calls' against the expectations and wishes of the they-self; it 'speaks' to you individually but tells you what you don't want to hear. This is where the folk-psychology of conscience as the voice of God or social conditioning comes from; people don't like the call of conscience, which is always inconvenient, and so disown it as coming from outside of them. Examining the lived experience of having a conscience, however, shows that the *caller* in conscience is *your own Being as the anxious potentiality-for-being from which you are hiding in everydayness*. You find yourself thrown as a particular person into a world where you must realise your potentiality-for-

88

being by actualising possibilities that are possibilities only because of your potentiality-for-being. You make yourself at home in this world by hiding in everydayness and belonging. Your conscience, however, manifests the uncanniness [not-at-home-ness] which is disclosed by anxiety. So the 'caller' of conscience is your own, alienated, potentiality-for-being which doesn't feel 'at home' in the world.

You must be careful here not to 'thingise' the caller as some sort of real you; doing that would go beyond what the evidence allows. Conscience is just the awareness that remains that, in fleeing, you are fleeing some aspect of you own potentiality. It seems 'other' than you only because the they-self has alienated itself from its own potential-for-being-authentic.

Understanding the Call of Conscience; Guilt. Conscience is everywhere associated with guilt. Human cultures ('they') normally attribute this guilt to having violated some sort of law. This attribution fails, however, to explain what it is about being-in-the-world that gives rise to the universal human notions of responsibility, law and guilt in the first place. As you might expect, from his analyses of being in space as emerging from our being-spatial, and being in time as emerging from our being-temporal, Heidegger traces our notions of responsibility [being guilty] to being-guilty.

Being-guilty is not a matter of having broken some moral code but is the sense of responsibility that explains why persons have moral codes. Just as Heidegger disclosed the Being of

89

both Care and conscience by looking 'through' the everyday differences that obscure them, in order to get at the aspect of being-in-the-world which explains them, so too he analyses the human notions of guilt to get at the aspect of being-in-the-world which explains why all human existence embodies notions of guilt and responsibility. What he finds common to all notions of guilt is **being-the-basis** of [being responsible for] a state of affairs which involves some kind of **nullity** [a negation, not, lack, absence, failure or something that we believe should not be the case]. If Heidegger's existential analysis of guilt is right (as it does seem to be) then the universality of conscience must attest to each of us being-the-basis of at least one nullity which is an *essential* part of our personal being-in-the-world as thrown projection. Thrownness and projection are both structures of Care (2.3) and, to explain a being-guilty, a nullity, for which we are responsible [being-the-basis] must attach to one or both of the structures of Care (i.e.,). As it happens, a nullity attaches to:

- The Nullity of Thrownness (Care being-towards the past) is the fact that what, who, where, or when, you are, matters to you and you didn't choose to be what, who, where, or when, you are. You simply awoke to there-being to find yourself already thrown into having to be yourself within a particular set of circumstances. This thrownness - which is a function of the past - is not of your making *but is your concern* - it matters to you. Being who and what your are, as a person in a circumstance, which is not your doing, must be 'taken over' and managed by you - you are not the basis of your existence but have to become its basis (who else is going to live your life for you?).

- The Nullity of Projection (Care being-towards the future) is the fact that being a potentiality means (1) always projecting yourself as *not* what you are being-towards and (2) that by actualising any one possibility you thereby waive other possibilities (the time spent at a job, for example, cannot be spent in other ways at the same time). You have to manage your being-towards the future as one who is concerned with, and liable for, what does not yet exist *and* what will never exist because of your choices.

It is, then, being landed with having to take over being-the-basis of our existence as thrown projection which gives us a sense of being landed with responsibility for our own existence even though we have done nothing to deserve such responsibility.

Our Being as Care is, in its very essence, permeated by nullity; with a 'mineness' standing on 'not mine'. And our primordial sense of responsibility [our sense of being-guilty] - to which conscience attests - has nothing to do with any kind of moral, political, or religious, failure. We tend to think it does only because, just as our conscience is fallen into average intelligibility (i.e., we cover over an awareness that authentic there-being is possible with feelings that we have failed some they-specific religious, moral or political code), so our primordial sense of responsibility is fallen into average intelligibility as social or religious guilt. The fact, however, is that being-guilty is more primordial than any religious, political, or moral, ideologies founded on it and it is this primordial being-guilty that conscience discloses.

Heidegger interprets conscience, phenomenologically, as a generally misunderstood call to exist authentically that is made by our potentiality-for-being authentic. 'Hearing' the call correctly amounts to having an understanding of yourself in your ownmost **potentiality-for-being-guilty**; that is, your own potentiality for becoming responsible for your being-in-the-world both as thrown and as projective. *You become aware of your own potential for existing as a real (authentic) thrown projection*. This is the attestation that we have a potentiality-for-being-authentic that Heidegger was looking for. It is the existential [lived over time] structure of authentic potentiality-for-being, attested to by conscience, which he now wants to 'lay bare' in order to disclose the authentic being-in-the-world which he wishes to interrogate to disclose the meaning of Being itself.

We have already seen that understanding is a matter of knowing what to do with an entity. Understanding the call of conscience entails a knowing what to do with your awareness that you are responsible for your existence as thrown and projection (a condition translated in *Being and Time* as '**wanting to have a conscience**'). In taking up responsibility for your own existence - as thrown and as projective - you disclose the being-in-the-world from which you have been hiding. In everydayness, the disclosedness of being-in-the-world is constituted by state-of-mind, understanding, fallenness, and discourse. If you take ownership of your own being-in-the-world, however, fallenness drops away and you disclose an authentic state-of-mind (readiness for anxiety), an authentic understanding (self-projection upon your own potentiality for being responsible), and an authentic discourse (reticence).

Reticence is a disinclination to join in or listen to 'they'. Where a they-self is all too willing to indulge endless idle talk, Heidegger predicts that the authentic self would be reticent [stilled by conscience].

It makes sense that an authentic being-in-the-world would commit to authentic discourse [reticence]. But being-in-the-world authentically would be difficult because we are all so deeply embedded in being-with 'they'. To break the grip of the 'they' - and thereby disclose the there-being that has been closed off by it - you would need to • 'hear' the call of conscience, • understand the significance of your own potentiality-for-being, • accept your own finitude and being-guilty, • be ready for anxiety, and • project yourself as Care on your actual [thrown] Situation *as it is* in responsibility for yourself and your actions (qv, *certainty* and *conviction*). This combination of understanding, acceptance, responsibility and reticent determination is 'resoluteness'. **Resoluteness** is a matter of acting as a responsible potentiality-for-being 'within the concrete situation' rather than letting fallenness, wishing or a 'they' dictate how you exist. As such, it is the authentic alternative to the normally irresoluteness [turbulence, qv] of being a they-self; you make up your mind about your values, and stick to them, rather than going along with whatever is convenient and/or popular. From the analysis of being-guilty, it could be projected that resoluteness would be a way of reticently [quietly or without fuss] projecting yourself upon

93

your ownmost potentiality-for-being-authentic, and exacting anxiety of yourself. It is a way of taking ownership of your own existence as it is, has been and will be. As such, resoluteness is an authentic being-oneself through the disclosive projection and understanding of what is actually possible at a time - it is, in other words, the way that we would exist were we not fallen.

To own your own potentiality-for-being in resoluteness is a matter of understanding what is actually possible and choosing to accept your responsibility for being who you are on *that* ground - even if that is no longer the ground on which you have been letting yourself be defined. This is (existing resolutely) is integrated with disclosedness because there-being is disclosedness and resoluteness discloses the authentic character of existence. Only by being-in-the-world authentically [resolutely] do you truly disclose your actual **Situation** (upper case 'S'); that is, the *definite* range of *actual* possibilities which become the world in which you are authentic. Existing authentically would be quite contrary to the kind of detachment from the world which many 'spiritual' superstitions teach - we wouldn't move 'out' of the world but from being lost in the they-world to being solidly located in the actual world. Resoluteness returns us to our *particular* (thrown) place in the world, to specific concernful relations with actual entities and solicitous relationships with actual other persons, where we can discover what our possibilities really are and seize upon them in a way that is authentically our own rather than as prescribed by 'they'. 'They' deal in abstracts, 'they' are always telling us what men are like, what women want, what workers think and clients need, and so on and on. Your Situation contains none of these types because it is limited to concrete actualities and possibilities. Existing resolutely would abandon the endless abstracts of 'they' for the reality of your Situation.

4. Temporality

Whereas time is a relationship between events, temporality is an activity - a person-generated process of temporalising, of putting events in a temporal order. Temporalising is, in turn, the condition or ground of what Heidegger calls the 'ecstatic' quality of temporality - its 'standing outside of itself [its own unity]' as past, present, and future. **Temporalising** is the process whereby persons both create and inhabit a unified past, present and future, as the horizon (qv) of being-in-the-world. This is something that we do in the process of living our lives as persons [plants and animals are in time but don't temporalise - a rabbit, for instance, doesn't calculate whether it has time to dig a hole, it just starts digging], and it provides a unifying horizon which holds our lives together - your past, present and future, are the horizon of your life.

If we think back to what has been disclosed about everydayness, we can recall that human there-being is disclosed in terms of existentiality, facticity, and fallenness. Existentiality is the fact that being-in-the-world is an ongoing process of actualising various possibilities for existing that you disclose as possibilities by projecting your potentiality-for-being onto them. Facticity is the fact that you have an inherited constitution and context which you carry with you and as which you project yourself in being-in-the-world. Fallenness is the fact that, because of your social embeddedness and desire to escape the burden of being-in-the-world for yourself, you normally define yourself in 'they' terms. Fallenness is everybody's normal everyday way of being a person. It is the unity, or integrity, of these three which constitute your Being as Care. Existentiality, facticity and fallenness, are, however, not enough to account for the wholeness of your existence unless you note the temporal element of each. To wit:

Your existence is being-towards the future (being-ahead),
Your facticity is being-towards the past (being-already-in) and
Your fallenness is being-towards the present (being-alongside).

The 'Time' part of *Being and Time* exactly expands the 'Being' part. The Being part analysed the Being of there-being as Care in terms of existence, facticity and fallenness; the 'Time' part discloses your Being as Care in terms of being-ahead, being-already in, and being-alongside. In each case the first (Being) and second (Time) tripartite structure exactly 'fits' with, and enables, the other - one in the world, one in time. Thus:

Future	existence	being-ahead	(in projection)
Past	facticity	being-already-in	(in thrownness)
Present	fallenness	being-alongside	(in being fallen)

Uniting all of these elements is essential to disclosing there-being as Care - especially given that the phenomena of death, conscience and guilt are, as phenomena of there-being, also all grounded in Care. This means that being-one's-self must be conceived existentially - as a temporal process of Care. Another way of saying this is that temporality is the basis of the unity of the Care structure; in other words, temporality is the meaning of Care.

Temporality as the Meaning of Care. Heidegger is after the meaning of Being. Meaning has to do with relevance of how something fits into the worldhood of the world. You disclose meaning of entities in the world by projecting your potentiality-for-being onto them. This projection not only discloses the Being of the entity but also your own there-being as a person.[18] The meaning of entities discloses their Being, but it is only because persons deal with Being that the question of meaning arises. This means that when we seek the meaning of Care - i.e., that which unifies your there-being as a person both at a time and over time - we are touching on the whole integrity of your being-in-the-world. Care is primordial, and when we inquire about the meaning of Care, we are asking what makes being-in-the-world possible. The answer, it turns out, is temporality.

The link between Care as an existential unity and Care as a temporal unity - the link by which temporality is the meaning of Care - is best disclosed in resoluteness because resoluteness has to do with understanding your Being as Care. This understanding in turn presupposes an openness to temporality because any resoluteness is being-towards a future character which you have decided to be as you who

---

18. All of your experiences of objects of attention are based on, and derive from, projections of your own potentiality - i.e., it is only because persons are in-the-world understandingly (they relate to the Being of object) that they experience objects both as what they are for and as meaningful.

have been so far.[19] To this linking of future and past, resoluteness further discloses the current moment of your existence and presupposes your openness to it; so the present is its existential context [its being-in-the-world].

It can be further seen here why authentic being-in-the-world, a condition from which we normally flee, can reveal the whole of your there-being as a person. The they-self doesn't own its choices and so doesn't disclose the temporality of knowingly choosing for the future, right now [in the present], as you have been up until this point. Authenticity entails resoluteness which, in turn, discloses a tripartite temporality (i.e., simultaneously being-towards the future, past and present).

To say that temporality is the meaning of Care is to observe that *your capacity for holding the past, present and future together is what makes Care possible*. Without your innate temporality, you couldn't be-in-the-world as an entity that Cares. Care, constituted of existence (the future being-ahead-of-itself), facticity (the past being-already-in) and falling (the present being-alongside), is how persons exist in such a way that things and events in the world matter to us. What this mean is that we couldn't exist as Care - as beings who, from a basis informed by the past, define their character by choosing present possibilities aimed at future states of affairs - if we

---

19. Note here that the 'as you have been so far' involves another 'not' for which you are responsible. This is because who you have been no longer exists except in your ownership of it.

didn't unite the past, present and future in the process of being persons.

The tripartite temporal unity of Care has already been disclosed as being-ahead-of-itself, being-already in, and being-alongside; these are your being-towards the future, past, and present, respectively (see *the Care structure*). So this is the essential link between *Being* a person and *Time*.

The unity of temporality is more radical than might first appear because, in your temporalising, the past, present and future do not come in a succession; the future is not 'later' than your 'now' and your past is not 'earlier'. Rather, they are all present in your experience at the same time. For a present sound to be part of a song, for instance, it must be integrated with what has been and what is to come (melodies exist *only* over time). This being the case, the present, past and future are, in effect, 'outgrowths' [ecstases] of your temporal unity. The **ecstases** of existential time are the future, past and present (taken together/ecstases or singly/ecstasis), seen as 'outgrowths' of the temporalising which there-being institutes just by being what it is. Although the ecstases of future, present, and past, actively pull us towards different temporal horizons, they 'stand out' from the primordial unity of the future and past in a present temporality (see *Appendix 5*).

What Heidegger describes in *Being and Time* is the unity of past, present and future as it is actually lived by persons. The common and artificial measures of time - clock time or historical dating - come after this existential phenomenon as socially useful adjuncts which, for all their usefulness, hide the true, existential, Being of temporality (i.e., temporality as it really is). We have conditioned ourselves to think of time as a kind of tape-measure made up of moments that we are alongside one at a time. But existential time is actually a lived unity of past, present and future which you create, within which you live your life as a person, and which unites your life into a whole. In other words, the categorising of events as past, present and future is merely something that you do with your temporality.

4.1 Temporality and Everydayness

Given the foregoing analysis, we should expect there to be authentic and inauthentic ways of disclosing our temporality. There are.

State-of-mind - A state-of-mind [mood] is being-towards the *past* because it discloses how you Care about what is already the case. The temporal ecstasis of the past is that of 'having-been'. **Having been** is your present being-towards relationship with your past and who you have been up until the present. There-being constantly is there as having been; you are the child you were in the mode of having been it.

Because the past is never dead for persons - you 'take up' who you have been into your present there-being and project it onto your possibilities for being who you will be in the future - your having been is part of your present (projective) Being. The extent to which you own or disown your having been is one of the measures of being authentic or inauthentic (see *repetition*, below). This is why your past is never lost or wasted. It is not uncommon for some people, who have gained a skill at some cost, to feel that their past learning is wasted if they find themselves in a situation where they can't use what they learned. What is flawed about this reasoning is that such a person still is that learner in the mode of having been her or him, so the value of her or his new existence is added to that of the old - the old is not subtracted because the past is still present in the person who was that learner.

Your having been is disclosed by your state of mind as an attunement to the facticity that arises from it. This disclosure makes it possible to discover facts about yourself and be 'brought back to' who you have been. What persons are 'brought back to' in a state-of-mind is a possible way of being a person that they can repeat [take up and adopt as their own again and again]. It is this possible repeatability that is the specific ecstatical mode of having-been. For the most part, however, your everyday having-been is a bringing back to thrownness in the manner of closing off (qv, see *forgetting*). Most moods, such as fear, hope, indifference, and so forth, are based upon this 'forgetting' mode of having-been. An example of this is the way that fear triggers inauthentic temporalising by being more animal-like than person-like. Consider, for example, a man who is suddenly threatened by an attacker. If this man reacts instinctively to what is there then any notion of authentic there-being is subordinated to the more urgent task of continuing to exist safely; questions about how he should or should not exist simply vanish. What we have here is the behaviour of an animal rather than a person; an action of instinct rather than reason. Such behaviour is perfectly understandable, but the point is that fear invokes inauthentic temporalising because someone reacting in a turbulent (qv) manner, rather than as a person, sacrifices authentic there-being to a more urgent present-tense need to simply go on living.

Contrary to states of mind like fear, anxiety provokes an authentic temporal grasp of your own existence as thrown into the world. In anxiety, you do not face a specific threat but potentiality and possibility which confronts you with the uncanniness of being thrown into the world as projective [as having to choose an existence]. As we saw in Chapter 2.4, that before which you are anxious is not encountered as something definite with which you can concern yourself. The threat does not come from what is ready-to-hand or present-at-hand, but rather from the fact that neither of these means anything in itself. The world in which you have existed is sunk into insignificance. When you find yourself adrift in a world whose contents have momentarily lost their involvement for you, two facts are disclosed; namely that (1) no fact dictates your existence and (2) you are already thrown into a world as projective and are thereby thrown into having to choose from among various possibilities. For this reason, anxiety embodies the authentic temporality of states-of-mind.

Understanding - Understanding is being-towards the *future* because you understand what it is to be a person only when you understand, however pre-ontologically, the role of possibilities in being-in-the-world. This corresponds to the being-ahead-of-yourself aspect of Care. The normal, inauthentic, human way of being-towards the future is one of merely awaiting it. **Awaiting** is a passive, and inauthentic, alternative to anticipation. **Anticipation** is a matter of actively 'meeting' the future in the present where, in awaiting, you simply let the future come towards you. You are, in effect, postponing your own potentiality-for-being. Persons will, for example, wait for the weekend or holidays or retirement, or a journey or whatever, as a time when they will really be able to 'just be themselves.' Their potentiality-for-being in these cases is not being-towards the future but simply waiting for a future to arrive.

Authentic temporalising anticipates the future right now, inauthentic temporalising merely awaits it; these two are different but, in neither case, does the temporalising go away. So your temporalising is disclosed even in inauthentic everyday existence.

Falling - Fallenness is being-towards the *present* in your everyday mode of being-alongside the world (i.e., your normal mode of inauthentic Care).

Fallenness is the normal human way of being-towards the present in which we are absorbed with our everyday lives and being with others. For the purposes of his temporal analysis of everyday fallenness, Heidegger focusses particularly on curiosity (qv). Curiosity, like fallenness as a whole, entails inauthentic temporality. Curiosity drives us from one present object of attention to another in a way that constantly consigns who we have been to a past that is of no interest. This is not because of the new object's relevance to your there-being but only because of its newness. Curiosity is thus an almost text-book case of a forgetting (qv) that 'makes present'. **Making present** is the inauthentic temporality in which we turn towards what is at hand - familiar, convenient or diverting - and away from the past and future. Addictions, and failing to keep inconvenient agreements, are classic symptoms of forgetting. In everyday curiosity, you tend to forget the past and future by engaging yourself with a possibility that catches your eye in the present.

In contrast with making present, authentic temporalising of the present involves 'now' being 'the moment of vision' - the time when you actively encounter your actual possibilities. **'Moment of vision'** is a phrase used by Søren Kierkegaard (1813-1855) to describe what the present becomes if you sight (qv) it as the location of actual possibilities and, therefore, of authentic choice. Treating the present as a moment of vision discloses the resources of your Situation both in their individual reality and their relation to your individual potentiality. This makes the present a time of resolution (qv) in which you find grounds for going forwards [being-towards the future]. You cannot be-towards the present authentically (treating it as a moment of vision) without simultaneously being-towards who you have been up until the present moment; you must own the past as something which is not under your control but still constitutive of who you are. What this amounts to is repeatedly coming back to the existence that you have chosen for yourself. This 'coming back' to a chosen existence is **repetition** - of being loyal to your past resolutions. If you are resolute then, rather than letting your self be tossed around by circumstances (qv, *turbulence*) you knowingly choose to keep repeating who you have chosen to be.

When you make a choice, in the present, you are being-towards the future (when what is presently a possibility will have become an actuality) as who you have been up until the moment of choice. Who you have been so far is the person who has been living your chosen existence. In everyday life both your existence and your character are substantially owned by the 'they.' But being resolute entails knowingly sticking by your chosen existence and character. This is not a matter of slavish conservativism but of understanding the process of there-being and owning the instance of there-being into which you have been personally thrown. If you are tempted by laziness, for example, but have resolved not to be lazy, then even keeping that resolve for years does not change the fact that being lazy is a possibility that remains open to you all the time. If you are being resolute then the present is an opportunity to repeat your past resolve - to 'hand it down' to yourself. This handing your resolve down to yourself is repetition. So repetition is a mode of resoluteness which hands itself down - the mode by which there-being exists explicitly as fate (qv).

4.2 Temporality and Historicality

History is the past made meaningful. You are always relating to history but can do so authentically or inauthentically (pretending that history is irrelevant relates to it inauthentically). As a thrown being, you are embedded in an historical circumstance by which some possibilities are open to you and some are not; being born in the 20th Century, for example, means that you can be an authentic car driver but cannot be an authentic Druid. This means that you inherit an historical context which dictates a kind of 'menu' from which you must select your possibilities for existence. Obviously you must 'read' this menu in order to understand your possibilities. This is difficult given that your inherited ways of understanding history is in terms of a 'they' interpretation. If you remain lost in thrall to 'they' then the best that you can do is inherit the destiny of your community. **Destiny** is the historically-determined facticity of a community that comes about because its structures and values are (a) shaped by the past actions and ongoing choices of its members and (b) determine the range of your own possibilities in much the same way as do your own individual past choices.

You cannot entirely escape the destiny of your community, but you can act resolutely within it. The resoluteness with which you exist authentically is a matter of taking personal responsibility for what you do with your historical Situation; you, in effect, 'take over' your past and hand it down to yourself as an inheritance. Our collective 'handing down' of our past to ourselves is the primordial basis of history as it is commonly understood (or, more correctly, misunderstood). Handing it down to yourself authentically gives you your past as fate. **Fate** is how the past constrains the present for those who authentically own their Situation.

Fate is always that of a specific individual, and never about a pre-determined future. The only determining force in fate is that of a having been which is part of your present character and Situation. Thus, to say "It is my fate to be faced with such-and-such a problem" does not imply any sort of extra-human agency or 'plan' - only that you are a finite being facing a world in which past events have resulted in circumstances with which you must now deal. Your past is fixed, but your fate - your confrontation with the past - is something you can variously accept, avoid, or distort. You grasp your fate once you own the thrownness of your Situation and act resolutely within it. An example of this would be someone who has been born into a despised race. The person who surrenders to this, in either apathy or violence, has no choice but to share in the destiny of her people. But the person who determines to decide her existence for herself, despite her thrown facticity, creates her fate for herself.

Now say, for instance, that someone born into a despised race determines to have a fate but, over time and with the weight of everydayness wearing her down, her resolve weakens (the lure of those possibilities that are closest at hand - comfort, shirking, and taking things lightly - tempt her away from resoluteness, see *forgetting*). To strengthen her resolve, she must, in effect, 'go back' to the Situation which gave rise to her resolution in the first place. She must, in other words, keep 'handing' *her* past down to herself. She mightn't like having to maintain her dignity day after day, year after year, but it is her 'fate' to have to do so if she is going to be an authentic person.

Your past-defined facticity has power over you. The 'powerless superior power' with which you face those facts is that of your freedom to do as you choose with what you have. You cannot, for example, change your birth facts - race, gender, social-historical context, genetic inheritance, and so on - but you can and do choose what to do with them. Your only 'fate' in this case is the Situation within which you exercise your freedom; it is this Situation which must be grasped resolutely if you are to exist [live the life of a person] authentically.

Only a person can have a destiny or fate because only there-being is innately temporal, and only temporal beings can grasp the past, in the present, while choosing for a future. Having a destiny is the default position for persons in everydayness; having a fate can be freed from having a destiny only by struggling (cf. *resoluteness*). Morever, it is the authentic grasping of the past - the acceptance of what it really means for the present and future - that constitutes the authentic historizing of it. Our capacity to choose how to exist - and thereby who to be - is real. Ironically, you cannot choose not to have that capacity or not to exercise it. Moreover, you have to exercise it in a world that you did not define and on the basis of a culturally-constructed understanding into which you are thrown. So your freedom as a person is rooted in a lack of freedom, and your power as a person is rooted in powerlessness. You cannot escape these constraints, but you can be an authentic person if you accept them resolutely (see *anticipatory resoluteness*).

Where resolute individuals have a fate, normal [turbulent] individuals can only have a destiny because the effect of the past on them is decided for them by their absorption in a community. This does not, however, imply that fate and destiny are entire alternatives; your personal fate is necessarily bound up with the destiny of your community - as the fate of ordinary folk caught up in economic, political or military turmoil demonstrates. Because being-with others is a necessary part of being-in-the-world, your authentic historizing includes a degree of co-historizing. The world you inherit is, after all, a social one in which the possibilities you inherit come down to us through various shared structures and practices. These possibilities are, moreover, typically taken up by us only with the cooperation of others. It is not possible, for example, to have a musical society unless lots of people maintain an involvement with music. And such a society can persist over time only if individual persons repeatedly choose to be involved with the possibilities it embodies (*repetition*, qv). If they do this authentically then they renew the vitality of these choices and, thereby, the culture of which they are a part. This means that any culture will persist in a vital way only so long as individuals grasp the possibilities chosen in the past and, if they don't, the culture will wither away. In short, your historizing is both an individual and communal affair and, to the individual, there corresponds a community; to individual fate, there corresponds communal destiny. So authentic historizing includes what Heidegger calls 'fateful destiny.'

This is as far as Heidegger got in his analysis of the meaning of Being. Some aspects of human being-in-the-world (notably language and technology) are dealt with in latter works - and there is quite a bit more to *Being and Time* than is touched on in this simple guide. All I wish to add, at this point, are some appendices concerning related issues.

*** * ***

Steven Foulds, New Zealand, February 2014
Feedback and questions are welcome steven@hinau.co.nz

Appendices

Appendix 1: Occidental Ontology. An ontology (qv) is a theory of Being. Everybody has an ontology, but most human ontologies are functional rather than theoretical; we simply act as if an ontology was true rather than thinking through its implications (most 'New Age' beliefs, for example, just fall down flat if you ask yourself what the world would have to be like for them to be true). The oldest, and still dominant, human ontology is dualism. **Dualism** is the ontological or pre-ontological belief that reality consists of two kinds of Being: the material [natural, objective] and the immaterial or non-natural [spiritual, cultural, mental, subjective]. This has its roots in ancient religion and probably arose from the uncanniness (qv) that early humans must have felt by being conscious of the world and, therefore, of being somehow 'other' than from the world (consciousness of the world entails consciousness that you are not the world of which you are conscious). In dualist conceptions of human personhood the 'essential you' is some kind of immaterial thing or substance - a soul, mind, spirit, or consciousness - that is materially embodied. A problem with this picture is that of explaining how the non-natural aspects of personhood - the spirit, soul or mind - fit into the natural aspects. This problem takes two main forms: **the mind-body problem** [how do mind and body interact?] and **the knowability problem** [how can the mind or soul, trapped within the body, really know that the world outside is as it seems to be?]. The mind-body problem is the 'rock and the hard place' of dualism and has still not been resolved by dualist philosophers. The knowability problem, which seems inescapable for dualism, led to what Kant called 'the scandal of philosophy' by which dualists (i.e., most humans) cannot prove the existence of an external world.

Some form or another of dualism is and always has been pretty much taken for granted by most humans - if only in their everyday way of talking (even materialists and idealists talk as if dualism was real). But the problems of dualism were not rigorously spelled out until the 17th Century when Rene Descartes (1596-1650) tried to address them. Descartes' *Meditations on First Philosophy* (published in Latin in 1641) is widely considered to be the beginning of Modern philosophy because it stimulated a immense and fruitful body of study and, virtually all Occidental[20] philosophy, from then until now, was and is, in one way or another, a response to the problems that Descartes brought to light and was unable to solve satisfactorily.

The philosophical issues with dualism, raised by Descartes, exercise philosophers to this day. One of the possible responses to the knowability problem is to simply (but implausibly) assert that you do not and cannot know that the world outside of you is as it seems, or even that it exists at all.

---

20. Although Heidegger limits himself to Occidental (Western) philosophy, Oriental (Eastern) philosophies face the same problems and fail to solve them in much the same way. Various forms of idealism, for example, have remained very popular in Hinduism and its offspring and face the same issues as led to the rejection of idealism in Occidental religions and secular philosophies.

This leads to scepticism and/or the rejection of dualism for idealism - which tries to maintain that only one of the two categories of Being in dualism is actually real. English-speaking philosophers and psychologists have, by and large, tended to reject idealism in favour of materialism and, at the time of writing, are still trying to reduce mind-talk to a materialist vocabulary. German-speaking philosophers, however, tended for some centuries towards forms of idealism that had been made plausible by Immanuel Kant's insights into the structure of perception and thinking.

Idealism is a deficient (qv) mode of Dualism which concludes that, because only the subjective/mental aspect of reality is knowably real, either only the subjective is real (ontological idealism) or, at least only subjective experience can be talked about as true (epistemological idealism). So idealism is actually idea-ism (the root is *idea* rather than *ideal*). Idealism 'solves' both the mind-body and knowability problems of dualism by rejecting the whole material/natural side of the dualist dichotomy as a construct of either the human mind ['subjective' idealism] or God's mind ['objective' idealism]. Nowadays idealism is most commonly found in various religions but, following the huge influence of Immanuel Kant (1724-1804), it became the dominant school of thought in Germany during the 19th Century.

Although a direct heir of the German tradition that followed Kant, and being very familiar with his thought, Heidegger was not convinced by German idealism and was more in the tradition of Husserl - who argued that dualism was flawed in dichotomizing consciousness [mind or soul] from the world just as if you could be conscious without conscious-of objects which, just by being objects of consciousness, constituted a world (see Appendix 2). In *Being and Time*, Heidegger replaces dualism with his observation that there-being is a being-in-the-world. This is a radical extension of Husserl (Heidegger saw Husserl's later works as smuggling a *de facto* dualism back into the interpretation of human Being). What is so radical about Heidegger's phenomenology is his uncompromising emphasis on being a person as an activity. All dualism explicitly or implicitly dichotomises personhood, as some sort of thing [mind, soul, Descartes' 'thinking substance', or whatever], from the world as another thing [matter, nature, Descartes 'extended substance', and so on]. Unlike other philosophers of the European tradition, Heidegger didn't tinker with this but rejected it. Being a person is an activity [project] undertaken in a 'workshop' [the world], and has to be-in that workshop in order to undertake that project (i.e., just to be what it is). On this basis he rejects the dualist dichotomy as misrepresenting of what is, in fact, a single [unified] phenomenon (i.e., being-in-the-world).

Appendix 2: Edmund Husserl (1859-1938). Edmund Husserl, who had a huge influence on Martin Heidegger both intellectually and personally, was the principle founder of the phenomenological method which Heidegger exploits and extends in *Being and Time*. The object of Husserl's method was to revitalise European philosophy by putting aside the historical-academic accretions with which it had become entangled and getting 'back to the things themselves'.

Considering an old issue with fresh eyes is not just a method of doing philosophy (or science) but also an attitude of mind. Over time, all inquiries tend to become bogged down with so much detail and history that more and more effort goes into achieving less and less. The difficulty with escaping this stultification is that it is not just the subject of inquiry that gets obscured; even your everyday experience of the world is ossified and distorted by what 'everyone' thinks, learns, and teaches. So escaping an inherited mind-set was very much a part of the phenomenological method.

The breakthrough concept, which enabled the phenomenological method, was the realisation that consciousness is intentional; that is, all your experiences of the world 'point at' [intend] real or imagined objects of some kind. One way of saying this is to observe that all consciousness is the individual consciousness of an object. For most of human history, humans have more-or-less taken it for granted that consciousness is somehow trapped inside of us and outside of the world. On this account, consciousness or the mind is a kind of empty box (Locke's *tabula rasa*) which could exist in an unfilled state [the 'pure, contentless consciousness' of some Hindu and New Age beliefs], persons somehow take to the world and fill with experiences by means of their senses or intuition, and can meaningfully be talked about, or even exist, as something abstracted from the concrete experience of an actual individual in a world. This assumption not only leads to all kinds of intractable complications but also ignores our actual experience. You have only to pay attention to your own being-in-the-world to notice that all awareness is awareness by you of something, all desire or fear is desire for or fear of something; your consciousness is not trapped outside of the world but concretely and irretrievably entwined with it. This essential 'of something' part of your consciousness is its intentionality. The intentional structure of consciousness was first spelled out in *Psychology from an Empirical Standpoint* (1874) by the German philosopher Franz Brentano (1838-1917).

Intentionality is the relationship whereby all consciousness is of some real or imagined object. Whenever you think about, fear, love, believe or desire, anything, the thoughts/feelings intend [metaphorically 'point at'] some real or imagined object of attention.[21] If you really were trapped inside your self and cut off from the world 'out there' then you could not explain how phenomena in the world affect your thoughts and feelings in the way they do. Disclosing intentionality, however, not only solves this issue but also shows just how inextricably you are bound up with being-in-the-world (your mind is not your home, the world is). Husserl's phenomenology focussed on the intentional experience which entwines us with the world. It puts aside metaphysical debates about what is and is not real, and epistemological debates about how you know

---

21. An **intentional object** is whatever a thought or feeling intends [is directed at]. If you desire chocolate, for example, then chocolate is the intentional object of your desire even if there is no actual chocolate in sight. Intentional objects do not have to be real - as folk who believe in 'the goddess' or have feelings for fictional characters demonstrate.

what is or is not real, to focus on simply describing the actual experience of being a person in the world.

Husserl's phenomenological method quickly revealed that persons enjoy or endure a radically different mode of Being from that of non-persons. We are not just things among other things - although we can be talked about in that way - because we relate to things in a way that they do not relate to us. You can desire chocolate, for instance, but chocolate doesn't desire anything. I am conscious of grass needing rain in a way that the grass itself is not conscious. In traditional philosophy, this difference gives rise to an artificial, and problematic, dichotomy between subject and object; you are here, inside your consciousness, the object is there outside of your consciousness. This dichotomy leads relentlessly to the conclusion that all that you can be sure of are the sensations in your mind, from which follows scepticism about the reality of the world. The 'subject' (you) is no longer an actual human person inextricably entwined with the world but a kind of abstract 'knower' who knows the world at a remove. Husserl's phenomenology sought to overcome this dualism by focussing on the intentional act whereby the subject is 'in' the world. When you are conscious of your computer, for instance, you are not conscious of an image in your head but of an object in the world. When you are conscious of being hungry then you are not conscious of an idea but of a sensation in your stomach.

The issue that Heidegger had with Husserl's phenomenology is that it didn't radically enough escape the dualist tradition.

Indeed, Husserl's 1928 *The Phenomenology of Internal Time-Consciousness* (which was actually edited by Heidegger), is virtually neo-Cartesian simply because Husserl took the consciousness of the subject for granted as consciousness is commonly understood within the dualist tradition. **Consciousness** is a self-aware awareness of real, imagined, actual, and possible, objects in the world. It is not some thingish essence. Being conscious is a way of relating to [being-in] the world that is always consciousness of some intentional object. In dualist theories all around the world, however, consciousness is reified as some kind of thing or an essence (and Heidegger avoids use of the concept for precisely this reason). Husserl did not interrogate the Being of the conscious subject herself. He simply began with what he called 'the natural attitude' without noticing that, in fact, there is nothing natural about it. The 'natural' attitude of your consciousness of the world is as much informed by 'they' culture as anything and everything else about human persons. The 'they' culture, in this case, was and is dualist - which explains why a neo-Cartesian dualism sneaks into Husserl's phenomenology despite his own best efforts. Heidegger is more radical than Husserl by using the phenomenological method in Being and Time to explore the Being of the conscious subject that Husserl's phenomenology had itself overlooked.

Appendix 3: Heidegger and the Nazis. For reasons best known to themselves, a number of folk seem to delight in missing the point of Heidegger's philosophy by arguing about how much or how little he supported the Nazis during his brief tenure as

Rector of Freiburg University in 1933 (at the beginning of Germany's 'honeymoon' with Hitler). On a scale of relevance to understanding the important insights of *Being and Time* (published in 1927), this issue is roughly on a par with the matter of how often or little he trimmed his moustache. I sincerely hope that any readers of this Guide to *Being and Time* have better things to do with their intellectual abilities than waste them on such irrelevancies.

Appendix 4: Heidegger's Method (Phenomenology). Phenomenology is a philosophical method, developed by Edmund Husserl (qv), of disclosing phenomena by describing them directly as they appear to consciousness (i.e., with your descriptions stripped of the theorising, intellectual prejudices, historical assumptions, and so on, which so often get between us and the things which we wish to disclose). **A phenomenon** [singular] is any thing, fact or occurrence which is detectable by human persons. The original Greek use of the term - which Heidegger invokes - was of 'that which shows itself in itself'; a hammer, for instance, is a phenomenon when encountered as a hammer (i.e., as a tool having a purpose). **Phenomena** [plural] are the totality of what lies in the light of day or can be brought to the light (qv). An important feature of phenomena is that they appear to us within a context of meaning that derives from the process of being-in-the-world. When you encounter a tree, for example, you don't simply sense a myriad of meaningless differences in light, shape and colour; you encounter the tree as an entity with a Being that is distinct from the things around it (a phenomenon in the phenomenological sense is that which shows itself as Being and as a structure of Being). The '-ology' part of phenomenology derives from the Greek *logos* which means 'discourse' (qv). So a **phenomenology** (as Heidegger understood it) is a true, Being-disclosing discourse about phenomenon.

In order to disclose phenomena directly, the phenomenological method requires that you put aside ['bracket'] all of your theories about the phenomenon in question and simply describe it as you experience. If the nature documentaries on TV were phenomenological, for example, then instead of mixing evolutionary theory and anthropomorphism with what is observed, they would simply describe what is observed. This would make them into discourse instead of idle talk (which is what they are in fact). As you have seen from what Heidegger observed about the phenomenon of being a person, phenomenological observation is not at all superficial but penetrating and very careful.

In phenomenology, everything you assert about the object of inquiry must be exhibited and demonstrated directly. Thus, to the extent that Heidegger's description of being a person is truly phenomenological, you should be able to confirm his claims from your own experience of being a person and without reference to special theory.

The purpose of using the phenomenological method is to revitalise your study of phenomena by putting aside your books, assumptions, and pre-existing theory, and returning 'to the things themselves'. Our understanding of phenomena is typically stultified by cliche and historical development which obscure [close off, qv] what is really going on. If you try to describe an experience, for example, most people (including professionally trained counsellors and the like) won't actually hear you because they are too busy trying to fit your experience into a category (male, female, Maori, Gemini, worrier, and so on). To overcome this - to look at the whole issue with fresh eyes, so to speak - Heidegger turned the phenomenological method onto the Being of persons.

Appendix 5: Temporality. You can get an idea of Heidegger's insight into temporality and the ecstases if you think of temporality as analogous with a triangle and the ecstasies [past, present and future] as analogous to the corners of that triangle. A triangle is three corners that 'point' in different directions but form a single integrity. Two lines at an angle to each other are not corners of a triangle unless they are joined together *as* a triangle. The corners are not added to the triangle after the event; a triangle doesn't 'have' three corners but *is* three corners that come into being as part of the integrity that they constitute as a triangle. Note also that:

Temporality is not the condition of being located in time, in the thingish sense of just being in the world as time passes, but as living in a way that unites [integrates], and involves a variously authentic or inauthentic awareness of, a past, present and future. This matters for interpreting being a person because your existence is in fact a mode of temporality [a way of being-towards the future, past, and present, simultaneously]. Temporality involves being in a unity of past, present and future. As a self, you 'will be' your future self, but only in terms of having been your past self; the past for persons is not merely past but still around. Selves, in other words, do not merely 'have' a past, you live your past; you exist on the terms that your past makes available to you. This 'going back' to what it has been [repetition, qv] constitutes, together with a simultaneous 'coming towards' the future and 'being with' the present, the unity of your temporality.

Temporality, as an essential aspect of the Being of there-being, is not some kind of external framework within which you just happen to exist. It is not, in other words, clock time or scientific time; you do not exist 'in' time but 'as' a temporality of 'done that, doing this, and am going to do the other'. This entails that human ideas of time (and history) are a product of our innate temporality and not the other way around (we are not temporal because we are in time but in time because we are temporal).[22]

The past, present and future are not three distinct 'things' but a single, integrated and living, phenomenon. This follows from the analysis of Care as a unity.

---

22. A person can disclose a sheep as living within a framework of time, but try imagining what it would be like to be a sheep with no notion of that framework.

Glossary of Heidegger's Terms Used in this Guide

Alienation - The normal everyday condition in which you are cut off from your own *potentiality-for-being* by (a) being *fallen* into the world and (b) the *average intelligibility* that goes with belonging to a community (a '*they*').

Ambiguity - The mixture of truth, half-truth and untruth in *idle talk*.

Anticipation - A response to our own *death*, as the impending and final end to potentiality, in which we • accept its *meaning* as our *ownmost*, *non-relational* and *not to be outstripped* and • begin to truly exist as *potentialities* for whom potentiality is radically limited.

Anticipatory resoluteness - An *authentic* way of there-being-in-the-world in which we ▪ face the ever-present possibility of impossibility with understanding (i.e., we *anticipate* death as impending, our ownmost, non-relational and not to be out stripped) and ▪ take responsibility for existing as potentialities within our 'concrete *Situation*' (the '*resoluteness*' part). A life of anticipatory resoluteness discloses the primordial temporality of Care.

Anxiety - The kind of uneasiness-before-uncertainty that arises from the way that possibilities in the world matter to you. The anxiety of which Heidegger writes is not fear (which is being-towards some object in the world). It is, rather, the more primordial *state-of-mind* which is concerned with the

125

lack of a sure foundation for your there-being. Although all animals can experience fear and stress, only persons experience anxiety because only persons have a Being of *Care* and *potentiality-for-being*.

Articulation - Expressing or pronouncing *the 'as' structure* of an *interpretation*. Articulation uses *language* and derives from *discourse* (from which language also derives).

the 'as' structure - (1) The relationship whereby an object is understandable ['*intelligible*'] as *ready-to-hand* for a particular purpose. The 'as' structure is one of *involvement* in a project, and the 'as' in question changes the interpretation. You could, for example, interpret a tree as possibly involved in the making of timber, aesthetic activities, equipment for climbing or shade, and so on. (2) The logic of *interpretation* whereby you *sight* an object as involved in *existence* in some way.

Assignment and Reference - The cultural and rule-governed relationships between a piece of *equipment* and various persons (the reference) and person-related in-order-to tasks (the assignment), within which it has meaning. The *worldhood* of the *world* is instituted as a web of assignments and references.

Attestation - When you attest to something you provide evidence for or stand as witness of the truth about a moot claim. In putting *conscience* forward as an attestation of our potentiality-for-*authenticity* - as he does - Heidegger is saying that the presence of conscience in persons is the evidence we all have that authenticity 'beckons' us.

Authenticity (authentic there-being) - A possible way of *being-in-the-world* that is not covered over with being *fallen* into the world and *being-with* 'they'. This way of life would be a matter of turning away from *idle talk*, *sighting* your being-in-the-world as *thrown projection*, and acting in an understanding of there-being as *potentiality-for-being*. Heidegger describes such an existence as entailing *reticence*, *anticipatory resoluteness* and *a willingness to accept anxiety*.

The terms translated as 'authentic' and '*inauthentic*' are not intended in any moral, religious or political sense. Their context is that of trying to uncover the Being of *existence* when that Being is obscured by tradition, being fallen into the everyday world, and being-with 'they' - which is not the Being that Heidegger wants to *disclose*.

Average Everydayness - That which is for the most part common to the ordinary life of human persons in their everyday situations. Heidegger does not want to make the common mistake of taking the time and culture with which he is familiar as providing a paradigm of understanding human existence in all times and places. So the 'average everydayness' that he *interrogates* are the ordinary *existential* structures of daily *being-in-the-world* rather then any particular historical/cultural variations of those structures.

Average intelligibility - The world of public opinion and understanding as a frame of reference which we all carry around with us. *Intelligibility* is the totality of *assignments*, *reference* and *significations* by which the world, its contents and history make sense to us. Average intelligibility is *levelled-down* by convention, popular opinion and *idle talk*. As such, it is the frame of reference [*horizon*] with which you are most familiar and by which you *interpret* the world.

Averageness - A characteristic of *being-with* in which *existence* is *levelled down* and homogenised, you accept a loss of self-ownership [*authenticity*] and your existence is largely interchangeable with that of other folk in your community. The more managerial you become, for instance, the more your daily existence is interchangeable with every other manager.

Awaiting - The normal, passive and *inauthentic* human way of *being-towards* the future. Where *anticipation* is a matter of actively 'meeting' the future, in awaiting you simply let the future come towards you. This difference is particularly disclosed in the way some folk anticipate *death* as an everyday possibility while others merely await it as a 'someday' eventuality.

Basic concept - The starting hypothesis or 'vague understanding' which initially founds a *circle of understanding* (cf. *fore-structure*).

Being - Heidegger's *basic concept* of Being (upper case 'B') is that (a) something is, and (b) is being as it is. The Being of a hammer, for example, is not just the fact that it 'is' but also its character, function, location (in space, time, and/or imagination) and way of being what it is. Being is always meaningful. Things, processes, and events, are *entities*, and Being is whatever captures that the 'are' in 'are entities'. A tree, for example, is an entity, and the Being of a tree is what the tree is when it is being a tree. This means that one of the ways of saying "What is a gate?" ("What is the Being of gates?") is to ask "What does it mean for something to be a gate?" Because the *meaning* of an entity is how it fits in with everything else in the *world*, the meaning of a gate is its character, place, and function, within an overall complex of the tools, projects and activities of gate users in the world.

   * Being is not anything mystical or otherworldly that is approachable only after extensive study and/or religious training. We all deal with Being all of the time. Every time you use a plate as a plate, or a spoon as a spoon, you are dealing with its Being.

   * Being is not a property. A gate, for example, does not 'have Being.' A welded steel structure can only be a gate if it is doing, or can do, what gates do when they are being gates (its Being has to do with the meaning of its function in the world). This entails that the Being of any object is always a function of its place and role in the scheme of things. So you cannot understand the Being of a gate, for instance, without reference to the role of enclosures and controlled movement.

   * There is no Being apart from some object of attention that is being what it is, and the Being of entities changes according to the entity in question. The Being of a tree, for instance, is different from the Being of, say, an idea or emotion. This means that the specific entity has to be examined to get at its Being. For reasons explained in the

Introduction to *Being and Time*, the life-long process of being a human person in the world is selected as the most appropriate entity to be examined ['*interrogated*'] in trying to understand the meaning of Being. So making the human way of being a person transparent to human persons quickly becomes, and remains, the theme of the text.

Being-the-basis - Being of cause, author or manager of a state of affairs; being responsible for. You are not the cause of your own circumstance [*thrownness*] and *existence* [projection] but have to be-the-basis [take over the management] of them *whatever they are*. This 'takeover' of inherited being-in-the-world which has, so to speak, been thrust on you, is what is involved in being-the-basis of your own personhood.

Being-ahead (**being-ahead-of-itself**) - The aspect of being-in-the-world which is related to *possibility* and your being-towards the future.

Being-alongside - Your normal, everyday, existence in which *being-in-the-world* as a *potentiality-for-being* is compromised by habit and the assumptions taken for granted by your community.

Being-already-in - The fact that you awoke to personhood to find yourself already in a *world* that is as it is.

Being-one's-self (sometimes, for the sake of linguistic felicity in this Guide, **being-your-self** or **being-a-self**) - The ongoing activity by which you are who you are over time and change.

At one time, for example, you were a tiny infant and then a small child, the only way in which you are the same 'who I am' now, as you were then, is not your body, history, memories or personality (all of which will have changed completely over time) but by always having been the same Self. This self-maintenance [*self-subsistence*] is being-one's-self. Being-a-self is a life-long activity which you personally undertake using '*they*' paradigms of *existence*, language, reasoning, and so on.

Being-guilty - Having a sense of responsibility arising from your *Being* as *Care*. Being-guilty - which is not a matter of being guilty of some wrongdoing but simply a fact of being a person - is the *existential* ground of ethics, guilt-talk and guilt-behaviour in persons. The fact that being-guilty is built right into *being-in-the-world* explains why persons have a *conscience*.

Being-in - The way in which persons behave towards the *world* which provides them with *equipment* for *existing* in one way or another. Being-in is way of relating to the world and its contents as meaningful (see the '*there*' of there-being).

Being in the truth - That aspect of there-being whereby you cover, uncover, discover or are mistaken about, the *Being* of entities. Being in the truth does not mean that whatever you believe is true but only that the *disclosure* of truth is an essential aspect of *being-in*-the-world. A tree, for example, cannot have false beliefs about itself or the world because it cannot have true beliefs about itself and the world. Persons, on the other hand, can have true or false beliefs about themselves, the world and each other. Being in the truth is an *existentiale* of being a person.

Being-in-the-world - The life-long activity of being meaningfully engaged with possibilities in the world as a workshop ['*wherein*'] of character-making - an *existential* (rather than *categorial*) unity which replaces the traditional 'subject/object' dichotomy as the basis of interpreting *existence*. Being-in-the-world is the fundamental and necessary existential condition of there-being. In the same way that you cannot be a driver without driving something, or a gardener without growing something, so you cannot be [exist as] a person without being-in-a-world.

    * Traditional notions of our being in the world detach us (as 'subject') from the world (as 'object'). This makes being in the world something secondary to being a person; you could describe either one independently of the other. This dichotomy may have its place in some human studies but does not apply to existence, for which being-in-the-world is a single datum.

Being-towards - An *essential* aspect of *being-in-the-world* whereby persons are always oriented towards various objects of attention that are of concern to their *existence*. There-being is always being-towards comprehendingly - i.e., unlike things, persons variously understand or misunderstand what their attention is 'pointing at' (see *intentionality* in Appendix 2).

Being-towards-death - The authentic or inauthentic way in which the *existence* of there-being is affected by being *thrown* into *death*. Being-towards-death is not the same as aging or dying, nor can it be reduced to an awareness that you are going to die, but is a way of life that owns or disowns the truth that your death • is yours alone, • makes being-with 'they' irrelevant and • cannot be avoided.

Being-with - The fact that *being-in-the-world* as a person always and *essentially* entails the input of other persons. The fact of being-with others is both inescapable and hugely influential on the project of *being-a-self*.

Care - A fundamental *existentiale* of being a person whereby facts, and the possibilities they represent, all matter to persons in various ways - you desire or fear them, value them highly, or couldn't care less. Care, which arises from the fact that *Being* is a *issue* for you, is expressed as, and explains, all the other aspects of your *being-in-the-world*. Care about things is *concern*, Care about persons is *solicitude*.

The Care Structure - The three-part *temporality* of simultaneously *being-ahead-of-yourself* [*existence*], being *already-in* the world [*facticity*] and *being-alongside* the world [*fallenness*] as the ways in which *Care* is *articulated*. It is the temporal Care structure that enables you to *exist* as a person in the world and over time. So say, for example, that you are desperately poor. In such a case, money is of *concern* to you. In trying to get money, you are being-towards who you will be after you have money (the future), as who you already are (a product of the past) in the world as it is (the present). Only by holding the past, present and future *together* can you exist as someone to whom money matters.

Category - A class of *Being* that applies to non-persons; e.g., the classes animate/inanimate, or none/some/all, are categories.

Categorial - The *interpretation* of what various entities are or are not it terms of which *categories* to which they belong. Traditional scientific description is categorial. Because thingish categories do not describe *existence*, the disclosure of being a person [there-being] must be *existential*.

Certainty - Primordially, certainty means being-certain as a state of Being; it is, in other words, a property of persons. To say that a state of affairs is 'a certainty' is derivative of this.

Circumspection - A way of being-in-the-world by being on the looking for things as potential *equipment*; the contrary to *reflection*. Being a person is circumspective because we do not sense all things equally but are always on the lookout for fact or possibilities that are relevant to our existence. Circumspection is interested *sight*; the kind of perceptual framework you get when you have a need or project in mind; it is not disinterested and not contemplative. The way in which superstitious folk are always alert to events that can be interpreted as supporting their superstition is an extension of this. Circumspection is related to *disclosedness* and is what turns seeing objects into perception [*sight*].

The Circle of Understanding - A process of gaining knowledge by starting with a *basic concept* which guides an inquiry, the conclusions of which refine or modify the basic concept into a new starting point for continuing inquiry.

Clearing - A metaphor for the fact that, just by *being-in-the-world* as *potentialities*, persons encounter and disclose *entities* as meaningful (a clearing lets in the 'light of understanding' and discloses Being). Because persons are in the world *circumspectively*, it is as if we each carrying a little pool of light' [an openness to understanding] with us as we go about existing. Because *understanding* is an essential aspect [*existentiale*] of being a person, you always understand or misunderstand *Being* where nonpersons do neither (to a cow, for example, nothing is cleared or closed off because cows do not encounter things in that way - *disclosedness* is not an existentiale of their Being).

Closeness (spatial)- An achievement in which you bring what is normally *remote* to your own attention by being *concerned* with possibilities that are relevant to your existence. Closeness is measured in terms of relevance rather than yards or metres.

Closing off - The contrary of *disclosing*. You close off the *Being* of *entities* off when you turn away from them emotionally (see *turning*) and/or cover them up with misunderstandings, half-truths, and/or false theory.

Community - *Any* group of persons who share common assumptions and/or ways of existing. Members of a community usually, but need not, share a location; there are, for example, professional, religious or life-style communities speaking different languages, but sharing similar ways of existing, in different countries all over the world.

Concern - Your relationship with objects in the world, including your own body and abilities, according to their relevance for your *existence*. Concern is the *existentiale* of *Care* as expressed concerning things (cf. *solicitude* for Care about persons). Heidegger's use of this word does not imply that persons are always concerned for objects but only that they matter to us in various ways.

Conscience - The suspicion, unique to persons, that we are responsible beings. What Heidegger calls 'conscience' is not just a feeling of discomfort at having offended someone or broken a rule but the more *primordial* phenomenon that explains the feeling. This phenomenon has to do with *Care* and *being-guilty* [being responsible].

Conscience as a Call - The way in which your *conscience* seems to summon you towards taking personal responsibility for your *existence*. This silent 'summons' reveals that you harbour a potentiality for living *authentically*.

Conviction - A form of *certainty* in which you let the testimony of 'the thing itself' - the *truth* of your real *Situation* - be the sole determinant of your being-towards it understandingly.

Curiosity - The search for novelty as a distraction from the burden of authentically *being-in-the-world* for yourself. Curiosity comes into play when *discourse* becomes detached from *truth* and attached instead to *idle talk*.

Dasein (**there-being**) - The way of *being-in-the-world* that is peculiar to persons. The German word literally means 'person' but is capitalised by Heidegger to stress that what he is investigating is not what persons are but how they go about the task of being a person in the world over time (the *Being* of persons is the activity of *there-being*).

Death - The end of *being-in-the-world*, that is; the end of your *potentiality* for *existing* in one way or another. Heidegger distinguishes the end of existence [death] from the biological *perishing* of your body, to bring out the *meaning* of death for persons. *Existentially*, your death constantly *impends* as the ever-present possibility of the impossibility of there-being when you finally and permanently 'run out' of possibilities for existing in one way or another. Existentiality, your death impends as your *ownmost*, *non-relational*, and *not to be outstripped*.

Deficient - Derived from a more *primordial* form. The experience of being alone, for example, derives from, and is dependent on, the experience of being in the company of others. This means that being with others is primordial and being alone is a deficient [derived] mode of *being-with*.

Deseverance (spatiality) - The bringing of something *close* in the *existential* sense. *Remoteness* is the default spatial relationship of persons and things in the world - you are 'severed' from them by your indifference - and de-severance is that part of the remoteness-closeness *existentiale* by which you selectively overcome your normal remoteness by your *concern* with only some possibilities for being who you are.

Destiny - The historically-determined *facticity* of a community; the communal equivalent of individual *fate*. Destiny comes about because the structures and values of any society or culture are shaped by the past actions and ongoing choices of its members and determine the range of your own possibilities in much the same way as do your own individual past choices.

Determine - To cause to have the character it does. If the nest-building of sparrows is determined by their species-structure, for example, then it is their species-structure that causes them to build nests in the way they do.

Detrimentality - The condition of something *ready-to-hand* being a threat, obstacle, or liability. A glue that gives off toxic fumes which cause headaches, for example, has detrimentality as its kind of *involvement*; so does a dishonest or incompetent accountant, a cowardly soldier, and an untrustworthy friend or colleague. The detrimentality threatened by events, possibilities, and other people, is what we fear.

Disclosedness - Uncovering or revealing the *Being* of *phenomena*. You disclose the Being of a tree or hammer, for instance, when you *understand* it as (a) 'fitting in' to, and having significance for, the 'overall scheme of things' which is the *world*, and (b) having certain possibilities for use in various projects that have to do with *existing* in one way or another in the world. A difference between you and a caterpillar that crawls over a hammer, for example, is that you disclose the Being of the hammer as equipment for existing whereas the caterpillar doesn't.

Discourse - A matter of persons talking with and listening to each other, verbally, pictorially, by gestures or in various printed forms, as a way of disclosing their own *Being* and the Being of entities which they encounter in the world. Discourse is not a matter of simply trading information [making *assertions*] but of making manifest the *meaning* of what you are talking about (qv, *disclosedness*). Discourse manifests itself in the narrative use of verbal, pictorial, or other, signs (i.e., it uses *language* as its equipment) and, together with *mood* and *understanding* discloses *being-in-the-world* to us.

Distantiality - Any differences, between yourself and a *'they'*, which threatens your acceptance by your cultural community. We decrease distantiality by conforming to various fashionable modes of attitude, jargon, dress and taste.

Ecstasis [sing], **ecstases** [plur] - The future, past and present (taken together or singly), as 'outgrowths' of the *temporalising* which there-being institutes just by being what it is. The use of this word captures that fact that, for persons, the future and past are an essential part of the present as we experience it.

As persons, we live in a unity of past, present, and future, from which the future, present, and past 'stand out' as offshoots or outgrowths (in the original Greek, 'ecstasis' [*ex stasis*] literally means 'standing [*stasis*] outside [*ex*]'). See *temporality*

Entanglement - An absorption with 'discovering' yourself as a thing. Entanglement shows itself in attempts to categorise persons by gender, race, psychological or astrological type, and so on. Like all other aspects of being *fallen* into the world, self-entanglement is a defence against the *anxiety* of having to choose your own *existence* for yourself.

Entity - Any object of attention which can be distinguished from another object of attention. All material things are entities, but so are immaterial objects of attention such as time, space or the activity of being a person; so the word 'entity' means more than just a material thing. All *Being* is the Being of some entity.

Environment - That part of the *world* which is most immediately around you in your everyday existence - your home, places of work, play, or socialising, etc. It is your environment that you deal with on an everyday basis.

Equipment - *Ready-to-hand* objects that are used or useful towards some end (eating, shelter, good works, sewing, writing, measuring, transport, crime, music making, building and so on) which ultimately has to do with a way of *existing*. A bed, for example, is equipment for rest, comfort, and/or intimacy; a holiday is equipment for rest and/or recreation.

Essence - That without which an *entity* could not be the entity it is. The essence of a non-person is its material structure. What is essential to being a person is a particular way of living in and relating to a world. This way of life is your *existence*. So, in Heidegger's terms, the essence of *there-being* [the activity of being a person] is existence.

Essential - Being part of something's *essence*. In modern English, the word 'essential' is often levelled down to mean 'important to.' But an essence is that without which an entity simply could not be the entity it is, and the word 'essential' is used throughout this page in its literal denotation of 'that without an entity would not be what it is'.

Existence - The way of life involved in the process of being a person [*there-being*] in the *world* over time. Existence is more than life because all that is essential for life are certain biological processes. The process of being a person, however, requires particular kinds of ongoing engagements with *possibilities*. This engagement [existence] entails relating to the world as a kind of workshop ['*wherein*'] for existing in one way or another.

Existentiale (sing; plural = **existentialia**) - A class of choice which applies only to *existence*. Being honest and dishonest, for example, are existentialia because only persons can and must choose to exist in one of these ways or the other.

Existential analysis - The analysis of *existence*. Existential analysis is to existence what categorial analysis is to things.

Such analysis is *ontological*, and spells out the meaningful structures [forms] of existence common to persons without specific reference to any one individual's way of life in particular (the analysis of a single person's way of life is *existentiell*).

Existentiality - The common lived structures [*existentialia*] that constitute *existence*. Existentiality has particularly to do with fact that your character as a person is realised by the process of living your life towards the future rather than being pre-determined by some essence or force outside of you.

Existentiell - Having to do with the particular existence of an actual individual in a particular circumstance. Dealing with possibilities in certain ways is *existential* (above) through being a universal fact of *existence*. The way that any one person deals with the specific possibilities of her or his situation is a existentiell fact of her or his existence. So whereas you can analyse the existential structures of there-being even for persons you don't know, an existentiell analysis of any given person's existence must await the evidence of that person's life.

Facticity - All the facts about you and your circumstances that are actual in the present because of past events and choices (cf. *thrownness*). These include natural facts such as your present weight, height, and skin colour; social facts such as race, class, and nationality; psychological facts such as your current web of belief, desires, and character traits; historical facts such as your past actions, family background, and broader historical milieu; and so on. You carry you facticity with you out of the past and into the future.

Fallenness (also '**falling prey to**', '**falling into**', etc.) - The fact of everyday *existence* being caught up in ('fallen into') everyday concerns, and historically established ways of being persons, to the extent that *being-in-the-world* is obscured. There are no moral, religious or political connotations to being fallen; it's just a fact of life that most of our existence is taken up with a daily round of communally-defined tasks, habits and rituals. By letting the inherited culture of a community define our daily existence, we lose sight of the fact that we are choosing a way of life and have to go on choosing that way of life every day of our lives.

Fate - How the past constrains the present for individuals who authentically own their *Situation*. The alternative to taking personal ownership of your Situation as fate is to be owned by the *destiny* of your community.

Finding yourself - Becoming aware of your own *being-in-the-world* that has been *lost* in *being-with* others; *understanding* and *interpreting* your Being as a person *existentially* (i.e., as it really is). Finding yourself is not a matter of going to a counsellor or travelling somewhere novel to 'look for' yourself but of disclosing the *being-one's-self* that you have lost sight of by letting '*they*' decide 'the tasks, rules, and standards, the urgency and extent, of concernful and solicitous Being-in-the-world'.

Finitude - The limits to your possibilities arising from your mortality, your circumstances, what you are [a particular human being], and the nature of world in which you exist (cf; *facticity*). These limits are variously logical, physical, psychological and temporal; you cannot, for example, escape death, the 'laws' of logic or nature, your physical limitations, or your social-historical context [the past]. The most fundamental finitude of being a person arises from the fact that every choice of a possibility thereby closes off the possibilities which are not chosen. You could, for example, exist for a million years, but every time you chose to, say, tell a lie in that time, you would thereby necessarily waive the possibility of existing as a truth-teller on that occasion. This means that your finitude is not primarily a product of a limited lifespan. It is, rather, simply a fact of being a person of any kind (even God would have to be finite in this sense because if, for example, He choose to reveal Himself to a person He would thereby waive the possibility of not having revealed Himself).

Fore-structure - The historical/intellectual background of an *interpretation*; a culturally-affected grasp of the *worldhood* of the world which you carry with you to your encounters with objects in the world. You cannot avoid having a fore-structure to all your interpretations of things and events; the best you can do is to try to be aware of your fore-structures and check them for flaws.

Forgetting - The everyday and inauthentic alternative to *repetition*; not a lapse of memory but a turning away from

144

who you have been in order to merely engage with something that just happens to be at hand. A classic instance of this is someone who gets sick or in trouble through a behaviour, promises herself never to behave like that again, and the forgets that promise as soon as a new opportunity to behave that way presents itself (acting as if promises haven't been made or don't matter is one of the most common symptoms of forgetting generally). Forgetting is a kind of repression of the past (having been) in which we not only repress an awareness of who we have been but also of the fact that we are suppressing an awareness.

For-the-sake-of (and **for-the-sake-of-which**) - The *existence* of *there-being* as the reason why *equipment* has its Being. Thus a hammer, for example, is usable *in-order-to* perform a task in the service [for-the-sake] of someone's *existence*.

Freedom (existential) - The ability to choose from among various possible modes of *existence* are open to you. All freedom is limited to the particular possibilities that are open to a particular person. Over-defining freedom, as a matter of simply being able to do whatever you want, overlooks the *facticity* into which you are thrown. The particular freedom attested to by *conscience* is the possibility of *being-in-the-world authentically* (a possibility which the universality of conscience attests to as being open to every person).

Freeing, **Freeing for** - The way in which the environmental context [*worldhood*] of something *ready-to-hand* allows its *Being* to be *sighted* - the worldhood of a plumber's workshop, for example, frees the equipment and materials in it to be understood as being there for the project of making gas, water, and waste management systems available to serve human existences. Similarly, the worldhood of certain art galleries frees pretentious trash to be seen as art.

Grounded - Confirmed or validated by evidential data and/or reasoning. Inquiry always begins with some sort of *basic concept*. If this concept is reasonably accurate then it will be grounded in evidence and reason as the inquiry proceeds. The beliefs carried by *idle talk* are ungrounded because they are adrift from the *being-in-the-world* which they purport to *disclose*.

Guilt - *Being-the-basis* of a *nullity* ['not'] about which we are concerned. The two primordial nullities for which we have to become the basis are *thrownness* and *projection*. Our *Being* as *Care* [concern, solicitude) is the foundation of guilt which is, in turn, the foundation of our notions of responsibility and moral or religious guilt (see *being-guilty*).

Having been - Your present relationship with your past and who you have been up until the present (there-being constantly is as having been). Right now, for example, you are the child you were in the mode of having been her or him.

the 'Here' - Your *place* in the world as a individual person - a place defined in relation to the '*yonder*' of relevant items and regions in the *world* as a web of *assignments* and *references*. If, for example, someone 'phones and asks "Where are you?"

146

it does not help to say "Here" - you reply in terms of 'at home', 'in the lounge' or 'at the game.' These places in the world (home, lounge, the game) are a 'yonder' from which you derive your 'here'.

History - The past as meaningful. *Historicality* is an extension of *temporality* by which we *interpret* past events in terms of their meaning as (a) experiments in possible ways of existing and/or (b) their influence on present ways of existing.

Historicality - The aspect of being a person whereby persons create a *history* (i.e., relate to the past as meaningful) just by existing as they have to if they are going to be persons at all.

Horizon - The meaningful framework within which certain entities are being what they are and/or various activities take place. An horizon is the limit of a *world*. In terms of time, the horizon of your life is the past as far back as you can remember and the future until your *death* - so your lifespan, at a time in history, is the temporal horizon of your existence. In terms of your nature, the fact that you cannot experience any point of view except your own means that your personal points of view over time provide the horizon of your experiences. The facts of yourself and your circumstances provide an horizon for your possibilities.

A **human person** - An animal of the species *homo sapiens* that is being a person (i.e., *being-in-the-world* as *thrown potentiality* that *Cares*). Although humans are *persons*, being human is not the same as being a person and not the subject of *Being and Time*.

In-order-to - The aspect of *equipment's significance* whereby you *understand* its *Being* in terms of what it is for. The Being of a hammer, for example, arises from the fact that it may be used 'in order to' build something, break something, or attack someone *for-the-sake* of someone's *existence*.

Idle Talk - Discourse in which what is said about a subject, and how it is said, takes precedence over the *true disclosure* of *Being*. Colloquially known as 'bullshit'. In idle talk you receive, discuss and pass on, what is said about a subject without checking the veracity of the claims. Idle talk takes on a life of its own which becomes increasingly detached from what it is supposed to be about. The claims of such talk then become the interpretations and half-truths which 'everyone knows' as you are 'delivered over' to them. Most of what you hear, say, read, or write, in your lifetime is idle talk or '**scribbling**' [the written form of idle talk]. This kind of verbal activity doesn't disclose the world so much as close it off by covering up Being with assumptions, half-truths, unsubstantiated claims, gossip, and conventional prejudice (see *ambiguity*).

Impend - To be possible at any time. For persons, *death* **impends** [looms over our lives] in a way that it doesn't for other living beings because we do not know when or how we are going to die but we do know (a) that we will die, (b) we could die at any moment, and (c) our death will be the end of our potentiality-for-being in this world.

Inauthentic - The normal human way of *being-in-the-world* in which we are caught up [*fallen* into] the everyday world and various communally-established ways of existing. The word is not pejorative but is a strictly technical term for describing the ordinary everyday kind of *existence* that obscures [*closes off*] the existential Being of *being-in-the-world* that Heidegger wants to interrogate.

Individualisation - The disclosure of your aloneness before the world as a particular *potentiality-for-being* who has to choose the possibility [*existence*] that will disclose *possibilities* for that existence to you.

Intelligibility - Understandability; the totality-of-*significations* by which you make sense of things (i.e., *interpret* them in the light of *assignments* and *references* which give them their *meaning* in terms of persons *being-in-the-world*).

Interrogate - Examine or analyse an entity *existentially* rather than *categorially*. When Heidegger interrogates the *Being* of human persons, for example, he examines our *existence* - not our biology, psychology or sociology.

Interpretation - A development of *understanding* in which you disclose the *in-order-to* connections by which an object serves [is *for-the-sake-of*] someone's *existence*. To understand a builder's hammer, for example, all you have to do is pick it up and use it. You interpret the hammer's *Being* if you comprehend it as belonging to a class of *equipment* that can be used in-order-to, say, build or repair a shelter. You would have to interpret a hammer's 'in-order-to' before you would know to put it in your tool box before you set out on a building project.

Issue - As issue is something of *concern* for you which is not yet settled. To say that any actuality or possibility is an issue for you means that it matters [is relevant] to your existence in a way that concerns you.

Levelling (usually levelling off or levelling down) - The kind of homogenisation that goes with belonging to, and fitting in with, a group of persons who are existing in similar ways. The qualifications '...off' and '...down' refer to the fact that levelling tends towards *averageness*, simplification, devaluation, and 'lowest common denominator' thinking.

Lostness - The fact that letting yourself, your life and your possibilities be defined by *publicness* loses *sight* of your Being as a *thrown* and *projective*. You simply exist as 'people like me' exist. '*Finding*' your there-being, is an alternative to lostness.

Making present - Caring so much about your immediate pleasure or convenience that you don't learn from the past, or keep past-made agreements, and ignore the future consequences of your behaviour. The everyday *being-towards* the present in which, by busying ourselves with what is immediately at hand, we merely happen to be there at the same time as our possibilities (cf. *being-alongside*).

Meaning - Where and how an object fits within the *articulation* of whatever integrity of involvements it plays a role.

Mineness - The fact that each and every instance of *there-being* belongs to a specific, concretely realised, individual. There-being is never abstract and never shared; there is always a particular person who can say, of any there-being, "This is mine and mine alone, no other person who will ever be who I am." Your *existence*, your *freedom*, and your *death*, are exclusively yours in this sense.

Mode - A structured way of being.

Moment of vision - What the present becomes if you *sight* it as the location of actual possibilities and, therefore, of authentic choice. The alternative to making the present a time [moment] of vision is to merely make it present (qv. *making present*).

Mood - An enduring/underlying emotional attunement to having been *thrown* into the world as who you are. Moods *disclose* your *state-of-mind* and, where *understanding* has to do with the future, states of mind emerge from the past (i.e., how you have experienced being thrown into the world so far). Moods are part of our *disclosedness* and *there-being* is never free of them; even apathy is a mood.

Nullity - Any meaningful negation [not], absence, lack or failure. A nullity may be an absence [lack], a contradiction, an inability, or simply some fact that is not there (a possible future, for example, is a nullity by having meaning but not yet being actual). Be careful not to over-define nullity as something mysterious; you are invoking Heidegger's sense of nullity any time that you use words such as 'not', 'never' or 'negative' in a meaningful way. Two nullities that play a significant role in being-in-the-world are *thrownness* and *projection*; that is, the fact that ∎ you are not the basis of your own existence, do not control the world, and ∎ have to constantly project yourself towards being what you are not yet.

Object - Short for 'object of attention'. Objects include things and events (*entities*), ideas, feelings, thoughts, memories, imaginings, actualities and possibilities.

Ontical - Scientific or pseudo-scientific inquiry which is devoted to the description of *entities* in terms of *categories* such as weight, size, mass, texture, psychological type and so on.

Ontology - An inquiry into, or theoretical belief that purports to explain, how *Being* is arranged. Because *meaning* is a matter of figuring out where something fits into the *world*, ontology is always finally about the meaning of Being. The dominant human ontology is, and always has been, *dualism*; that is, the belief or assumption that Being has both natural and non-natural [spiritual, mental, or cultural] forms (see Appendix 1).

Ontological - Having to do with the fundamental and *meaningful* Being of things. *Being* is meaningful only to persons [*there-being*] and only in terms of its relevance to *existence*. All ontical studies, such as the sciences, pre-suppose an ontology. Even an ontical description of clothing, for example, simply does and must pre-suppose an ontology that imputes meaning to various items of clothing. This ontology is 'prior' to the ontical study because, without it, the ontical study could not distinguish between kinds of entity. Ontically, a shirt is described as having certain physical features (size, shape, colouring, texture, etc). Ontologically, is has a meaning that is related to a way that someone goes about the business of being a person in the world. It is this meaning that makes it a shirt rather than something else (i.e., the ontological meaning is its Being). In pre-supposing an ontology, all ontical studies pre-suppose the Being of the activity [being-in-the-world] for which ontical studies are a possible way of life. An inquiry into this Being would be ontological because it explores the ground on which the ontical inquiry stands. The issue that Heidegger had with traditional ontological inquires is that they are 'blind' by not having a clear idea of what Being itself is. It is this blindness that he hoped to cure by his ontological investigation into the Being of human persons.

Others - Beings who are not you but like you in ■ being neither *ready-to-hand* nor *present-at-hand* and ■ *being-in-the-world*. Just as *there-being* is never without a *world* so is it never without others (see *being-with*).

Ownmost - Inescapably yours and yours alone (cf. *mineness*). Even when you are existing inauthentically, your pain and *death* are your ownmost.

Non-relational - Making you relationships with other folk and your community (including your standing in a community) irrelevant. Your *death* is non-relational.

Not to be outstripped - Of *death*, the fact that you have to die your death for yourself.

Perishing - The end of biological life as contrasted with the end of *existence*. Heidegger makes a distinction between perishing - which all living entities come to - and *death* [the personal end of someone's specific *being-in-the-world*] as a way of bringing out the *Being* of death which is obscured by the everyday, and inauthentic, conflation of death with perishing. Just as the existence of persons differs from the lives of plants and animals, so too does their death.

Person - A living entity, with a *potentiality* for *existing* in different ways, that exists in the *world* over time. Called *dasein* (*there-being*) in German; being a person is an activity that involves choosing a way to exist from among possibilities (a cat, for instance, cannot be honest or dishonest whereas a person can be either and must constantly choose which one to be). Although being a *human* and being a person coincide on this planet they are not synonymous. Folk who believe in gods, angels, spirits and/or aliens, believe that such entities are persons without being human.

Personhood - My term for the collection of behaviours or facts that constitute a *person*. Traditionally human personhood has been interpreted *categorially*. In *Being and Time*, Heidegger interprets it *existentially* (which makes far more sense).

Possibility (categorial) - A state of 'could be but isn't yet'. As a category of *Being* applied to things, possibility is grouped with actuality and impossibility.

Possibility (existential) - An aspect of *existence* whereby persons are always *being-in-the-world* as possible builders or destroyers, possible saints or slobs, possibly cruel or kind, and so on. The *categorial possibilities* of things derives wholly from the existential possibilities of person (e.g., the possibility of a rock as a building material derives from the possibility of persons using rocks to build with). Existential possibility is called '*potentiality-for-being*' (qv).

Potentiality-for-being - The potential, to be any one of a number of possible persons, that arises from always having more than one possible existence that you could choose. You always have, for example, the potentiality-to-be a gambler by choosing a gambler's existence, the possibility to be loving by choosing a loving existence, and so on. As with *possibilities*, your potentiality-for-being is limited but real. It is because of your potentiality-for-being a number of very different characters that Being is an *issue* for you, you *Care*, you have to be engaged with a world, and you integrate the past and the future in your present being-in-the-world. Potentiality-for-being contrasts with *facticity* - which is your actuality as an already-defined being. The hyphenated phrase potentiality-for-being intends a primordial and defining feature of being a person as always being something more than its present facticity.

Potentiality-for-being-guilty - Your potentiality for of accepting personal responsibility for your *existence*.

Pre-ontological - The normal human condition in which we make *ontological* distinctions even though we lack a coherent *ontology*. In your everyday life, you distinguish between persons and things, or the real and imaginary, in such a way that, if someone treats a person as a thing, a real object as imaginary, or vice versa, then you rule their behaviour as confused. So someone who fell in love with a hammer, for instance, or who 'parked' her children in the garage, would stand out to you as having her ontological categories awry - a judgement which indicates that you have at least some pre-ontological understanding of such categories even if your ontology is not fully thought out and/or incoherent.

Present-at-hand (presence-at-hand) - Something that is in the world but of no immediate relevance to what you are doing (cf. *ready-to-hand*).

Place - Where something belongs in the spatial arrangement of your environment. Place is *existential*, not *categorial*. So the place for kitchen utensils, for example, is in a kitchen (which is, in turn, a *region* set aside for the performing of certain undertakings).

Primordial - Most primary or fundamental. Knowing how to feed or amuse ourselves, for example - how to tend goats, drive cars or work in a shop - is more primordial to *there-being* [more immediately involved in your being persons] than is having theoretical knowledge about nutrition, agriculture, mechanical engineering or retail marketing and so on. Similarly, *ontological* inquiries are more primordial than *ontical* inquiries by being about the foundations on which ontical inquiries stand.

Projection - An *existentiale* (qv) of *there-being* by which persons understand the *possibilities* of objects by, in effect, 'shining' the light of their own *potentiality* onto them (cf. *clearing*). Humans, for example, discovered the possibility of making fire, by rubbing certain kinds of wood or by banging certain kinds of rock together, by projecting their potentiality for making and using fire on various entities around them. The sense of the word is related to that of 'projectile', the projection of light into the darkness, projecting your voice toward the back of an audience, and a person or organisation projecting its influence into an area of interest. Because possibilities become actualities only after you project your potentiality onto them, projection is always *being-towards* the future.

Publicness - Your internalised social conformity [*averageness*, *distantiality*, and *levelling* down], which controls the way in which *being-in-the-world* gets *interpreted* by you. Publicness is the set of social assumptions, beliefs and attitudes which dictates *existence* in ways and to an extent of which you are normally unaware.

Ready-to-hand - Things, events, persons, and situations, that are relevant to someone's *existence* either as a help or as a hindrance (e.g., things, events, spaces, etc., that you can work with or which are obstacles to a project). The *meaning* of entities that are ready-to-hand is defined by their relevance to existence. An area of land, for example, may be ready-to-hand in relation to its actual or possible use as a building site or, if it is unstable, as a threat to roads or buildings (cf. *assignment* and *equipment*).

Region - A place in the *world* that is set aside for sets of related activities. In the way that persons organise the world as a 'workshop' of character-making, a region is a 'zone of operations' or 'whereabouts' ['*whither*'] assigned to a related set of activities - e.g., a kitchen, workplace, home, school, or marketplace (cf. *place*).

Remoteness (spatial) - Your normal spatial relationship with objects in the world in which you are detached ['*severed*'] from them because they are not of immediate interest to what you are doing.

Repetition - A re-choosing of previously chosen character values. If you are *resolute* then, rather than letting your self be tossed around by circumstances (qv, *turbulence*) you knowingly choose to keep maintaining who you have chosen to be (see *self-constancy*).

Resoluteness - *Existing* as *thrown potentiality-for-being* 'within the concrete *situation*' (BT 349); an essential aspect of existing as a potentiality rather than letting fallenness, wishing or a 'they' dictate what you do with your potentiality. Resoluteness is a way of '*reticently projecting* oneself upon one's ownmost *Being-guilty*, and exacting *anxiety* of oneself'. As such, resoluteness is an authentic existence through the *disclosive* projection and *understanding* of what is actually possible at a time - it is, in other words, the way that we would exist were we not *fallen*.

Reticence - The authentic contrary of *idle talk* (qv). *They-selves* are confident only because idle talk is adrift from the strict discipline of having to adhere to *truth* that is properly grounded in the being-in-the-world. Because authentic persons would lack this false confidence, it can be predicted that they would be reticent - cautious, inclined to reserve judgment and 'hang back' from idle talk or scribbling.

Seeing - Sensory detection without understanding. Fish, for example see; persons both see and have *sight*.

The **Self** - Whatever-it-is that maintains itself as the same *being-in-the-world* over time; not a 'soul', 'mind', personality or consciousness. Your self is *characterised* by your *history* and personality but cannot be reduced to either. Selfhood [being your self] is essentially *temporal* because it *subsists* as the same self over time and change (see *self-constancy*).

Self-constancy - The fact that each of *self* maintains itself as a particular self over time. Your body, circumstances, personality and attitudes may change considerably over time but the life-long project of *being-in-the-world* remains your self's *mine* over those changes. As an old man the 'I' that I indicate in self-reference has a very different historical, moral, physical and psychological character from the 'I' that I indicated as a child or young man, but is still the same self.

Serviceability - The appropriateness of a *ready-to-hand* object, or another person, for the project to which it/she has been, is, or can be, *assigned*. For example, a hammer's ability to drive nails into timber gives it a *towards-which* that makes it relevant *in-order-to* build a wood-framed shelter; this makes the hammer serviceable for the assigned task. What equipment serves in serviceability is the existence of a person or persons.

Sight - Seeing-with-understanding as a metaphor of all *circumspective* awareness. You may see thousands of entities during the day but you sight only those which are relevant to your *existence* in some way (see *ready-to-hand*). Sight is meaningful by being informed by *worldhood*. Sight, in other words, *discloses* what is there in terms of its *Being* - which has to do with its possibilities for use by persons.

Significance - Relevance or importance. The significance of objects in the world is always related to *existence* and disclosed by understanding ■ what they are for [their '*for-the-sake-of-which*'] and ■ how they fit into the overall arrangement of *assignments* and *references*. This is why an events may have huge significance to some folk and no significance at all to others.

the **Situation** (upper case 'S') - The definite range of actual possibilities into which you find yourself *thrown*. Your Situation is your *environment* shorn of they-narratives, idle talk and wishful thinking; it is the environment in which you *exist authentically*. You are not the ground of your Situation; it is always already there as the ground on which you find yourself existing (see *already-in*).

Solicitude - The range of *Care* attitudes that persons have towards each other. Solicitude includes such modes of Care as love, indifference, friendship, disliking and hatred (you can be uncaring or anti-caring towards other persons only because you can be caring; a cyclone or tree, on the other, is neither caring nor uncaring). Care is itself composed of considerateness and forbearance.

    <u>Considerateness</u> - The set of Care attitudes towards other people that ranges from caring deeply about their interests to being totally indifferent. Considerateness is an *existentiale*, which means that all of your attitudes towards other folk are always more or less considerate - always somewhere on the scale of loving to hate to indifference.

    <u>Forbearance</u> - The set of Care attitudes towards other people that ranges from tolerance to intolerance. Forbearance is also an *existentiale* and your attitudes towards others are always more or less tolerant.

Spatiality - The aspect of *being-in-the-world* whereby persons arrange the *world* [the 'workshop' of there-being] in much the same way that, in *temporality* they arrange the work of *there-being*. The existential spatiality of there-being is organised according to the relevance various entities have for your *existence*. *Existential* spatiality is not to be confused with the *categorial* space of science.

State of mind - That aspect of *being-in-the-world* whereby how you have so far experienced being *thrown* into the *world* is *disclosed* by your emotional 'attunement' to it. Your state of mind is disclosed by the *moods* which reveal how you feel about being you in your circumstances. Where your emotional state of mind discloses you being-towards the past as thrown, *understanding* discloses your being-towards the future as *projective*.

Subsistence - The *activity* by which by a *self* (a *entity* with the character of *Care*) maintains itself as the same self over time.

Temporality - The way that persons *temporalise* [order or arrange] events into a before, during and after (past, present and future) sequence which forms an *horizon* for existence. Being a person is an ongoing process of presently exploiting possibilities for the future as who you have defined yourself by your past choices. To do this, you must integrate the future and the past with the present as a unity. Temporality is not simply a matter of being in time but of simultaneously being-towards the past (as thrown), future (as projective) and present (as fallen). This means that the Being of persons can never be accurately interpreted 'out of time'; that is, as any sort of free-floating 'soul' or 'pure consciousness' or whatever.

Temporality as the Meaning of Care - The fact that your capacity for holding the past, present and future together is what makes *Care* possible.

Temporalising - The process whereby persons both create and inhabit a unified past, present and future, as the *horizon* of their *being-in-the-world*.

Temptation - The ground of *fallenness* that is itself prepared by *idle talk* and the way things have been publicly *interpreted* by '*they*'. Temptation is a predisposition to fallenness that arises from our *being-with* others and desire to escape the burden of personhood.

The '**there**' - *There*-being is the way of *being-in*-the-world that *discloses* the *Being* of ▪ objects in the world, ▪ the world itself and ▪ being-in-the-world. The 'there' of there-being is not a geographical location but the disclosive nature of existing (i.e., *there*-being is the kind of being that discloses things around it as meaningful). When Heidegger wishes to talk about geographical location he uses the terms translated as 'here' and 'yonder'.

'**They**' - The set of communal values to which you conform in fact (and usually without noticing that you are doing so); the undifferentiated 'everyone' in "Everyone's doing it" or "Everyone's got one"; public opinion; the social norm or 'done way of doing things' which determines your behaviour and your understanding of your possibilities.

They-self - The *self* as it *exists* when *fallen* into everyday life and lost in the '*they*'. The existence of a they-self is, in effect, owned by 'they'. Virtually all of us are being they-selves for virtually all of the time.

Thrownness - The fact of finding yourself landed with the task of *existing* as someone you didn't choose to be in a geographical, social, and historical, *world* that you didn't choose and don't control. The notion of being thrown into the world does not imply that any external being, beings, or force, placed you in the world for some purpose. All it captures is the fact that no one starts being a person except as some particular person in a particular circumstance. You don't get to go 'behind' your thrownness to choose a *Situation* that you find more congenial; you simply awake to personhood to find yourself pitched into a game you don't understand, as someone you didn't choose to be.

Thrown projection - The dual nature of being a *potentiality* who has to *project* possible ways of *existing* onto the actual world into which you find yourself *thrown* as who you are. Being simultaneously thrown and projective is your nature as an integrity of actuality and possibility by which you must realise your own *potentiality-for-being* as whoever you happen to be and from within a state of affairs that is actual and not of your making.

Towards-this - The aspect of *equipment*'s *significance* whereby you *understand* its *Being* in terms of its assigned relationship with related equipment. It is towards-this relationships that you trace when working out the integrity of *assignments* and *references* that constitute the *worldhood* of equipment.

Towards-which - The part of *equipment's Being* that is disclosed in terms of its having an assigned purpose within the totality of equipment. Towards-which is related to a tool's *serviceability* for a given task. For example, a hammer's ability to drive nails into timber gives it a towards-which function that makes it relevant *in-order-to* build a wood-framed shelter - it makes the hammer serviceable for the assigned task. The towards-which of equipment derives from the *being-towards* of the persons who use equipment in the service of their existence.

Truth - A 'two storey' bye-product of persons being *disclosive*.

1. The 'foundation' of truth is being-disclosive as the way in which persons *exist*. *Being in the truth* and disclosing truth are part of *there-being* because persons are beings to whom *Being* is an issue and who therefore disclose Being (see '*there*').

2. Secondarily, truth is the *Being* of entities that is disclosed by the disclosive 'there' of there-being disclosive. This is the truth that has to be disclosed before propositional truths can be true or false. Truth, in this sense, is a disclosure of Being by persons and *untruth* is an obscuring [*closing off*] of Being. Because the Being of entities is disclosed only by the *projection* of *potentiality-for-being* onto them, truth is not

normally apparent but has to be 'brought to light' by persons being-in-the-world.

The common philosophical concept of truth, as an agreement between words and what the words are about, is actually a *deficient* (tertiary) concept that comes into play only after truth in the second [disclosure] sense has been *asserted*.

Turbulence - An instability of *existence* that follows from being defined by ever-changing group dynamics rather than *resolutely* owning your own existence for yourself.

Turning (turning away, turning towards) - A metaphor for the two primordial attitudes or 'emotional attunements' that you can have towards having so far experienced being *thrown* into the world. Your *moods disclose* how you feel about having-been thrown into the world so far by 'turning' towards a fact or facts of your thrown *Being* and 'turning' away from it or them.

Uncanniness - The disturbing feeling of not being 'at home' in the world which is normally hidden by being *fallen* into the world and *being-with* 'they'; a translation of the German word 'unheimlich' [literally 'un-home-like', usually translated as 'spooky' or 'eerie'] as a description of how *being-in-the-world* would feel to someone who was existing *authentically*. Uncanniness is normally disclosed to us only when us when our everyday existence is stripped of its normal possibilities in moments of *anxiety*.

Understanding - A matter of being able to use an item as *equipment* for some project that has to do with realising a possible *existence*; you understand a garden, for example, not when you know the physics and chemistry of plant growth, but when you know what a garden is for and how to use it in a way that serves the project of being kind of person you are being. This means that understanding is not the end product of an intellectual process but your immediate and practical [pre-intellectual] grasp of objects as possibilities for existing in one way or another. Where *mood* discloses the past, understanding is always being-towards the future.

Untruth (falsity) - The *closing-off* or covering up of *truth*. If you fail to grasp the true *Being* of an entity, it is not the case that you grasp nothing but that you grasp an untruth (i.e., you misinterpret the object as something that it isn't).

Usability - The practical purpose for which *equipment* is *assigned* within a project. If you are using a glue to repair a toy, for example, the project of repairing the toy the *towards-which* that defines a glue's *serviceability*, while sticking various materials together is the for-which of its usability.

Wanting to have a Conscience- A possible mode of *authentic existence* in which you would accept responsibility for your own *Being*, *existence*, and character. We all are, in fact, *being the basis* of our own thrown existence. Wanting to have a conscience simply accepts ownership of that fact.

'**Wherein**' - The 'home' of an activity. A kitchen, for example, is the 'wherein' of preparing food to eat (see also *region*).

'**whither**' - An area in the *world*, as a 'workshop' of self-making, that has been assigned to certain projects. Kitchens, for example, are the 'whither' [region for food preparation] in which *equipment* for preparing food has its assigned *place*.

The **World** - The existential 'workshop' of character-making within which persons go about the task of *existing*. Things in space and time are made into a world by the way that persons *assign* roles to entities in the process of existing in one way or another. Worlds are always meaningful to persons.

Worldhood - A widely ramifying and integrated complex of roles, concepts, projects, *assignments*, *references*, *significance*, functions and functional interrelations, that arises from the fact that persons care about objects in the world for the possibilities with which they present us for existing in various ways. The worldhood of a hammer, for example, is that entire web of concepts, assignments and activities within which a hammer has its *Being* as *equipment* with an assigned function. The worldhood of the world is what makes the things around us cohere as a meaningful integrity [a world]. It is also what allows and invites us to encounter objects as *ready-to-hand* or *present-at-hand*.

Yonder - The objects in our *environment* to which we spatially relate when locating ourselves in the world (e.g., the assertion

"Margi lives in the Waikato" locates the '*here*' of Margi in terms of her relation to a 'yonder' that is the Waikato valley).

Index

172

CPSIA information can be obtained at www.ICGtesting.com
Printed in the USA
BVOW06s1322270716

457059BV00009B/20/P